A GUIDEBOOK TO CONTEMPORARY ARCHITECTURE IN MONTREAL

Second edition

A GUIDEBOOK TO CONTEMPORARY ARCHITECTURE IN MONTREAL
Second edition

NANCY DUNTON
HELEN MALKIN

WITH AN ESSAY BY
GEORGES ADAMCZYK
AND A CONVERSATION BETWEEN
RICARDO L. CASTRO AND MARTIN HOULE

DOUGLAS & McINTYRE

16 17 18 19 20 5 4 3 2 1

Douglas and McIntyre (2013) Ltd.
PO Box 219, Madeira Park, BC, V0N 2H0
www.douglas-mcintyre.com

Published simultaneously in French by Les Presses de l'Université de Montréal under the title *Guide de l'architecture contemporaine de Montréal* (ISBN 978-2-7606-3628-6)

Cataloguing data available from Library and Archives Canada
ISBN 978-1-77162-111-3 (paper)
ISBN 978-1-77162-112-0 (ebook)

Texts: Nancy Dunton
Cartography: Eric Leinberger
Photography editing: Alain Laforest
Research: Christine Boucher
Drawing preparation: Solange Guaida/ Alessandra Szekut

Book design: George Vaitkunas
Typesetting: Shed Simas
Cover and full-page photographs: Alain Laforest

Printed and bound in China
Printed on acid-free paper

Distributed in the US by Publishers Group West

Canada Council for the Arts   Conseil des Arts du Canada

Canada

Douglas and McIntyre (2013) Ltd. acknowledges the support of the Canada Council for the Arts, which last year invested $157 million to bring the arts to Canadians throughout the country. We also gratefully acknowledge financial support from the Government of Canada through the Canada Book Fund and from the Province of British Columbia through the BC Arts Council and the Book Publishing Tax Credit.

The authors gratefully acknowledge the financial support of the Canada Council in the preparation of the book.

Additional thanks go to the authors' families, friends and colleagues for their thoughtful comments and unflagging support.

CONTENTS

PREFACE

Why this book?

People who like to look at buildings like nothing better than being turned loose on a city with a good guidebook. After years of looking at contemporary architecture in other cities, it was frustrating not to be able to do so in one's own city. It was more frustrating still to not be able to hand a visitor that good guidebook and some metro tickets and send him or her out to see what Montreal had been building in the last thirty-plus years.

There is good architecture in Montreal. There are flashes of more than good; there are moments that are effervescent, and that's what makes Montreal so intriguing.

Why these buildings?

We selected buildings that we believe were well designed and possess an enduring quality, but equally, we asked ourselves whether the building had made a significant impact on its *quartier*. Had a project created new public space or contributed to civic life? Had it changed the way buildings were perceived in that neighbourhood? Did it use materials in an innovative way? Did it do a lot on a restrained budget? Does it transcend the time in which it was built?

Montreal is a city very vulnerable to economic cycles and to political events, so sometimes the reason why a building stands out is because of the time in which it was created. As Montrealers, we remember the recession of 1991–92, or we think of how audacious a gesture Usine C was – partly because nobody was building anything in the post-referendum deep freeze of 1995.

Sometimes what makes a building noteworthy – or visit-worthy – is that it asserts itself relative to those around it; and sometimes it's the obverse of the coin – a building makes itself known by quiet assurance.

Having a stock of interesting 19th-century buildings is one of Montreal's great assets; finding uses for them other than those for which they were intended is a skill that has been learned. Almost half the projects in this book about contemporary architecture intervene in existing buildings – they reuse, recycle, convert and add on. Some may now look a little dated, or even timid, by 21st-century standards, but their value derives in part from how innovative they were in their time. The best, of course, have that ineffable quality of timelessness.

University buildings and cultural institutions represent the majority of building types in this guidebook. Built as a way to inject money into the economy or – in the late 1990s – as the consequence of considerable individual donations to institutions, they have significantly changed the urban landscape of Montreal.

Neighbourhood-scale cultural buildings have proliferated in the 2000s. Design Montréal organized architectural competitions for four libraries and a cultural centre in different Montreal boroughs from 2009 to 2014, bolstered perhaps by the expectations generated by being named a UNESCO City of Design in 2006.

The Montreal housing type – the three-storey rowhouse with a common wall between it and its neighbours, and set back only by the width of an exterior staircase – is strong and ever-present in the city. Against this rich background, many of the most successful contemporary residential projects are those that declare themselves confidently as a type apart. It is unfortunate but true that a lot of the most recent condominium construction is not as successful as earlier insertion projects, so there is a very small number of condominiums included.

Hotels, restaurants and retail interiors are not included in this book because, of necessity, they change so often. Since 1995, Commerce Design Montréal has promoted and published the best that the city has to offer in this, the most ephemeral type of design project.

Are there projects that should have been included but have not? Perhaps. While much effort has gone into rigorously assessing each project according to the criteria outlined above, the ultimate choice is subjective. As well, of course, the limitations of time (a project had to be completed to be included) and space imposed themselves.

Why this time period?

The 1983 construction of Maison Alcan marked a shift in attitude, a shift towards a respect for the city and a connection to it that was for the most part absent in the 1970s.

A greater public consciousness of Montreal as a whole in the 1980s – influenced by major architectural competitions and public consultations – affected the next generation of architects to graduate from the city's two schools of architecture. The projects in this book are, for the most part, the work of that generation and of those who taught them.

The eight years since the first edition of this guidebook have been good ones for architects in the city – one of the longest stretches of building in many years. This has meant worthy additions to the book, particularly public spaces, but what is equally interesting is what's coming: a panoply of projects intended for completion for Montreal's 375th anniversary in 2017.

Who was this book written for?

Architects and designers, certainly, but more generally, people with an interest in and a curiosity about architecture. Implicit in the task that we set for ourselves – to write two hundred words about a given building – was the idea that the visitor standing on the sidewalk understood why a particular building was included.

The purpose of this guidebook is to allow the user to find buildings and places, and to discover something about them, to understand them in the context of Montreal's neighbourhoods. The projects selected represent what we would take visitors to see ourselves, what we would not want someone to miss.

Put the book in your pocket, get on the metro and go look at Montreal.

HOW TO USE THIS BOOK

Buildings and places in this book are all accessible by public transportation. Checking on hours and frequency of service of the bus and metro system is always advisable, at www.stm.ca. There are both public places and private houses in the guidebook, and every attempt has been made to be clear about access to buildings, but respect for privacy has been, and we believe should remain, paramount.

Projects to see are grouped according to *quartier*, or neighbourhood – the names correspond to those on the city maps in sidewalk kiosks and in metro stations. A short text about each gives the visitor a sense of the neighbourhood, but there is, of course, much more to see and explore.

The sequence of *quartiers* within the book starts from the downtown core and moves in a spiral towards the east, then loops back to the west. Maps of *quartiers* are oriented towards nominal Montreal north – to a Montrealer, St. Laurent runs north-south and Sherbrooke east-west. (This perception is so ubiquitous that it actually appears on some architectural drawings.) Representation of *quartiers* is based on historic and municipal definitions, though sometimes relaxed to show more of the context of the city. Metro stations are indicated by the metro symbol located at the most convenient entry point. As some stations have many entries, checking the metro system's neighbourhood map in the particular station may be useful.

The language of Montreal is French; most buildings are known only by their French names, so that is how they are titled in the book. When a building, exceptionally, uses both an English and a French name, the English version is given. Street names, both in texts and on *quartier* maps, correspond to city maps and street signage, to make finding one's way about as easy as possible.

Images of projects are typically, but not exclusively, those that the architects themselves use to present their work and, in most cases, show the project as it was at the time of completion. We are endlessly grateful to all the architects and photographers who responded to our requests for drawings and images.

Architects are identified by the name that the firm was known by at the time of project completion, as are clients. Indexes at the end of the guidebook are organized by building, by architectural firm and by building type, to allow for cross-referencing.

MONTREAL ARCHITECTURES

Georges Adamczyk

For many years described as a city sitting on the border between America and Europe, Montreal is now a global city, in the only French-speaking province of North America. Buffeted by waves of immigration and municipal annexations, mergers and de-mergers, the limits of the city have shifted. However, its spectacular geography remains, little changed from the descriptions found in the accounts of the early explorers. First and foremost, Montreal is a majestic island in the St. Lawrence, about five hundred square kilometres in area. Above the riverbanks looms Mount Royal, named by Jacques Cartier in 1535. Both a gateway to conquest and a commercial centre, the port spurred the city's growth from its founding in 1642.

At the beginning of the 20th century, the monumental architecture of banks and insurance companies rivalled with the industrial architecture of enormous grain elevators to transform a colonial city into a multicoloured collection of lively streets and avenues. The island of Montreal now has about 1.9 million inhabitants within a vast metropolitan area totalling more than 4 million. Even before setting out to see its contemporary architecture, visitors immediately sense that Montreal is a welcoming city. Walking through its neighbourhoods – each one so different and so lively in its own right – one sees the contrast between their vernacular brick rowhouses and the grey stone of the old city and the glass and steel that dominates the downtown core. The visitor quickly grasps the strong sense of place that Montrealers feel, which sets the city apart from others in North America. On the one hand, one is astonished by the excessiveness and the ambition of the built environment; on the other, charmed by the modesty and discretion of things.

How are these extremes combined in Montreal's contemporary architecture? The question can provide a measure for the poetry of expanses and materials that have influenced efforts by Montreal architects, as much as have the realities of uses and seasons. Let's turn first to history, to the drastic changes of the last few years and the aesthetic and social effects that have modified the horizon of architectural creation. This is the subject of this architectural guidebook, which presents with an inventive attitude the most significant and the most publicly accessible Montreal buildings.

The early 1980s marked an important moment in the history of urban development in Montreal. According to many observers and critics, this was the end of post-war modernism. The post-war period in Montreal saw the development of a new downtown, the glory years of international architecture and the opening of the city to the entire world with the 1967 Universal Exposition, and with the exorbitant 1976 Olympic Games. It was also the time of Quebec's Quiet Revolution. From 1950 to 1980, the spaces and landscapes of Montreal were radically transformed. Undoubtedly, this period bears a similarity to the decades at the end of the 19th century and the start of the 20th, which saw the dawn of modernity and the beginnings of an American identity for a city that had been French, then British. However, the post-war period was, more importantly, the swan song of modernism, which gave us unique buildings, rich in remarkable innovation. Today, unfortunately, we limit our appreciation of this time to a few architectural icons. Among these celebrated buildings, every self-respecting cosmopolitan guidebook will mention Habitat 67, the U.S. Pavilion, Place Ville Marie and the underground city, Westmount Square, the Tour de la Bourse (Place Victoria) and Place Bonaventure.

The early 1980s was the onset of the postmodern period. French philosopher Luc Ferry's analysis of postmodernity suggests three trends: postmodernity as high modernism; postmodernity as revivalism – returning to tradition as opposed to modernism; and postmodernity as going beyond modernism, threatening to overtake reason, potentially to find the end of art. Contemporary architecture is primarily characterized by the first two trends, though architectural thinking has also been affected by the crisis in art. Montreal's principal Canadian rival, Toronto, chose high modernism. In contrast, Montreal did not seek to intensify its modernist heritage. Moreover, it was even less prone to dash in front of the lights shining on the hypermodernist stage to take part in the pathetic deconstructions with which it is cluttered. Instead, Montreal can be identified with the second trend. The city fell back on a vernacular tradition, the architecture of its past, and rejected a modern architecture that had itself become the academic tradition.

This attitude of resistance did not reject creativity, but it did oppose the violent aspects of urban development that tended to destroy everything in the name of progress. Abandoning the search for universal values promised by modernism, by society in general – and architectural production in particular – was motivated by a dualistic cultural process of recognition and appropriation. Consequently, the preservation and reuse of built heritage gained a momentum that was only equalled by that of popular enthusiasm for the increase of Quebec's autonomy within Canada. Maison Alcan, designed in 1983 by Arcop, is the best symbol of this turnaround. These architects, renowned for the Brutalist aesthetic of their projects, shifted architectural innovation toward a dialogue between the contemporary value of new construction and the heritage value of existing buildings on redevelopment sites. Going beyond the categorical opposition that sociologist Manuel Castells noted between "renovation by bulldozer" and "conservation-recycling," henceforth it was more a matter of a culturalist approach to urban planning and a contextual approach to architecture in Montreal.

Reshaping the urban form – and especially the reconfiguration of accompanying public spaces – is seen by many observers as the concrete beginnings of the re-conquest of the city by its residents. This is the best place from which to appreciate the renewal of architecture. It is also a good way for visitors to make contact with Montreal's contemporary designers.

During the 1970s, the issue of how to redevelop surplus port properties arose, with attempts to impose an imperious urban development that lacked any consideration for the historic values and public interest of this unique site. Following an exemplary public consultation and an international ideas competition, in 1991, architects Cardinal Hardy, with Peter Rose and Jodoin Lamarre Pratte et Associés, proposed a development plan for this large site. The Old Port site was divided into two design areas: on the east, the Bonsecours Basin sector; on the west, the Locks sector. Inarguably, here history informs the composition of architecture and landscape, whether pre-existing or newly created. The development plan becomes an interpretive strategy. The peak years of harbour use – 1930 to 1960 – were the main reference, though there are also allusions to previous centuries. As visitors move through the site, they can easily identify traces of the first broad wharves along de la Commune. Whereas the East Sector is a place where plantings and structures formally display and analogously evoke the image of an active port, the West Sector offers a large worksite of industrial archaeology open to the public. Here, the composition is more narrative and provides visual emphasis to the entrance to the Lachine Canal and the restored locks. At the foot of the Silo No. 5 complex stands the Maison des Éclusiers, a well-designed, modest building that skilfully develops an architectonic lexicon inspired by industrial artefacts.

The Montreal Science Centre opened in 2000 on the King Edward Pier. Developed by the consortium of architects Gauthier Daoust Lestage/ Faucher Aubertin Brodeur Gauthier, this project follows the interpretive strategy established by the Old Port development plan. With great simplicity, a parallel pair of large hangars was recycled, one into the Centre, the other primarily for parking. Applying in almost subliminal fashion the principle that a building is a strict composition of its program, structure and envelope, the architects applied an extremely formalist, almost minimalist, rigour to these building. As a result, the gigantic scale of the project is forgotten. On the inside, the structure is perceptible, easily comprehended; thus, a visit to the Centre offers both a lesson in techniques and an architectural pleasure. Another remarkable building links the Old Port to Old Montreal: the Musée de la Pointe-à-Callière, especially the *Éperon*, or spur, designed by Dan Hanganu in collaboration with Provencher Roy and constructed in 1993. The solid presence of this building and its slender tower create a metaphor for ongoing history. The cylindrical form evokes the grain elevators; its masonry recalls the typical building material of the old city; its modern lines are supported by a classical composition. All of this melds the past and the future with a kind of found innocence – a rare quality in architecture.

The Cité Multimédia and the Quartier international de Montréal are two major urban redevelopment projects that have greatly contributed to the emphasis on a return to sources in the historic city and its *faubourgs*, the original suburbs. The transformation of the Faubourg des Récollets into the Cité Multimédia furthers the debate on the contemporary city and the world of research and experimentation in new technologies. The architecture of cables and wireless networks has diffused through the architecture of the city. As a unit, this old abandoned industrial district was recycled to house cutting-edge software companies. However, this is far from the temples of high tech. The tight network of city streets, the narrow blocks with traverse lots sufficient to accommodate several projects, completed and under construction – all have appropriated the language and appearance of Montreal buildings of the industrial age.

Among the many projects, two stand out for the quality of their execution. The first was completed in 1998 and received the Grand Prix d'Excellence of the Ordre des architectes du Québec. Architects Annie Lebel, Geneviève l'Heureux and Stéphane Pratte of Atelier in situ recycled the Weir Marine Outfitters Building for Discreet Logic and Behaviour Entertainment. The second is a new building, Édifice Louis-Charland, designed by architects Menkès Shooner Dagenais/Dupuis LeTourneux in 2001. Marking the entrance to downtown, it plays in two scales: that of the metropolis and that of the *quartier*.

The master plan created by the architectural consortium of Gauthier Daoust Lestage and Provencher Roy for the Quartier international de Montréal is a highly sophisticated urban project. The plan shaped all elements – lighting, street furniture, public art, street design – to ensure a strong sense of identity for the district. The project is very contemporary in appearance. In its public spaces it offers an image likely to respond to the demands of a cosmopolitan clientele, one that travels frequently and whose tastes are attuned to globalized sensibilities with regard to space and forms. It is easy to fall for the clichés of supermodernity and create sophisticated non-places, such as airports, convention centres, shopping malls, hotels and office buildings. They can be found all over the world and are often designed by the same major international architectural firms.

But Montreal is not Singapore, nor Dubai. The location of the Quartier international, between the downtown core and Old Montreal, called for a local, referential approach to the architectural context; the result successfully meets the challenge.

In addition to Place Bonaventure and the Tour de la Bourse, which define the western boundary of the Quartier international de Montréal, three projects contribute to its distinctive identity. The first of these was completed in 1991: the Centre de commerce mondial linked a number of existing buildings by adding a public corridor, the Ruelle des Fortifications, interiorized under a grand glass structure. All the period façades were conserved, and the additional buildings of the complex were inspired by the architecture of St. Jacques, for many years Montreal's financial and banking artery. Led by architects Arcop Associés and Provencher Roy, this hybrid project has become the contact point between the Quartier international and Old Montreal.

The second, the design of the expansion to the Palais des Congrès, was the result of a controversial competition won by an architectural consortium of Tétrault Parent Languedoc / Saia Barbarese Topouzanov / Aedifica with Hal Ingberg. The architects provided a strong concept, much of which is based on the tectonic qualities of the construction and, particularly, on the use of coloured glass for the new façade on Place Riopelle. In addition to integrating the 1983 convention centre building by Victor Prus, which rises above the Ville-Marie expressway trench, the new project encompasses historic buildings on St. Antoine. Moreover, it completes the underground network linking Place Bonaventure and Place des Arts. The project also provides vast east-west and – more importantly – north-south urban corridors. These corridors improve the link between Old Montreal and the rest of the city.

The third project, the Centre CDP Capital, is by architects Gauthier Daoust Lestage and Faucher Aubertin Brodeur Gauthier, the consortium also responsible for the Montreal Science Centre. The headquarters of the Caisse de dépôt et placement du Québec, this 2003 building reconnects with the modernist theme of the curtain-wall via its innovative building envelope. The structure occupies the entire block between McGill, St. Antoine, Place Riopelle and Viger. A long glazed *passerelle* links Place Riopelle to McGill St. It connects the rear façade of existing buildings on St. Antoine with the new building on Viger. Although this strategy is reminiscent of the Ruelle des Fortifications component of the Centre de commerce mondial de Montréal and Calatrava's BCE Galleria in Toronto, its intentions go further. An emphasis on bioclimatic functionality has led to high-energy performance in the complex. In keeping with their approach, the architects provide a composition that is literal, practical and economic in appearance, while efficient and elegant in terms of technical decisions.

Horizontality dominates in each of these projects. The permeability of places and their spatial linkage promote a reshaping of the urban form and the creation of innovative public spaces. No skyscrapers, no acrobatics and a complete absence of extravagance. Based on a concern for architecture's concrete qualities, the recognition of uses and their creative diversity, Montreal architecture is now well connected to the "Montrealness" described and defended by architect-critic-artist Melvin Charney.

The first experience of contemporary Montreal architecture must, necessarily, be followed by impressions of performance spaces. A city where language and speech are highly important, Canada and Quebec's cultural metropolis, Montreal is above all the artistic capital of Quebec. The Conseil des Arts de Montréal, founded in 1956, is the oldest arts council in Canada. In the 1980s, several international art events were born here, including the Festival International de Jazz de Montréal, the Festival de Théâtre des Amériques (now the Festival TransAmériques), the Festival International de Nouvelle Danse and the Cent Jours d'Art Contemporain (now the Biennale de Montréal). In addition, the city hosts the "Just for Laughs" Comedy Festival, the FrancoFolies, the World Film Festival, the Festival du Nouveau Cinéma and the Festival International du Film sur l'Art. Many of these events offer activities in public spaces, creating a succession of temporary installations. The Quartier des spectacles project around Place des Arts was essentially conceived to bring the ideas of the event and of the temporary – that ephemeral quality – to urban design. And not to be forgotten, the 1980s was also the time when street performers introduced the entire world to the Cirque du Soleil. Each of its new creations is presented under a big-top tent in the Old Port.

Montreal's insistence on artistic vitality is because of a desire to encourage visitors to explore the new venues for artistic productions. The architects of most of these small performance halls were able to show restraint in expression – but precision and vigour in the execution – while meeting the needs of the work and the audience. Théâtre du Rideau Vert, Théâtre d'Aujourd'hui, Cinémathèque Québécoise and Usine C by architects Saucier + Perrotte; Espace Go by FABG; Espace Chorégraphique Jean-Pierre Perreault by architect Pierre Thibault – each is astonishing in the simple and restrained way it distances itself from the spectacular exhibitionism so fashionable today. Other examples of cultural architecture's resistance to the globalizing stampede that visitors should see are the Grande Bibliothèque and the Canadian Centre for Architecture. On a much larger scale than the performance spaces mentioned above, these two designs respond to their expressive mission with assurance and integrity. They are both part of Quebec's cultural landscape, to be sure, but each is undeniably of its location, one in the east, one in the west. Both convey a justifiable mistrust of the flights of monumentalism that claim to be inspired by democracy.

The last few years have seen many remarkable projects for the construction and reconstruction of public spaces in Montreal: Place des Festivals, Square des Frères-Charon, Place d'Armes, Square Dorchester, Benny Park and Promenade Smith, winner of an architectural competition organized by the City of Montreal. It is precisely these City-organized competitions in architecture, and urban and landscape design that have promoted the design of buildings as original as the Bibliothèque Marc-Favreau by Dan Hanganu in Rosemont and the spectacular Stade de soccer by Saucier + Perrotte on the edge of the immense former Miron quarry. In addition to these projects, which are revitalizing working-class neighbourhoods, new urban places are emerging, such as the industrial enclave of Marconi-Alexandra. Visitors are invited to wander through the streets of this atypical part of the city in the full throes of transformation and renamed Mile-Ex. A multitude of new projects abounds: industrial spaces converted into lofts that settle in with the industries that continue to resist their demise and with urban housing projects, modest in size but audacious and innovative in design and materials.

In an attempt to conclude this introduction, which is still too short to do justice to the critical, exciting work accomplished by the authors, it occurs to me that we can take inspiration from Umberto Eco. We can approach Montreal as an open architectural work. It is also a city that celebrates minorities, a kind of minority city. Consequently, it is often in a minor key that architecture is expressed, though this does not exclude major results. Two minor projects – Jacques Rousseau's Maison Coloniale (1990) and the Jardin des Premières Nations pavilion, designed by Gilles Saucier and André Perrotte (2001) – are noteworthy for their meaningful intensity; they carry us away with subtle allegories on humanity's efforts to build and inhabit a land that must also be preserved.

Parc du Mont-Royal
Redpath-Crescent
Cedar
des Pins
du Docteur-Penfield
Côte-des-Neiges
Simpson
Redpath
du Musée
de la Montagne
Drummond
Stanley
McTavish
Montreal Museum of Fine Arts, Claire and Marc Bourgie Pavilion
Sherbrooke
Montreal Museum of Fine Arts, Jean-Noël-Desmarais Pavilion
Maison Alcan
Lincoln
Métro Peel
Métro McGi
De Maisonneuve
Métro Guy-Concordia
du Fort
Saint-Marc
Saint-Mathieu
Sainte-Catherine
Tupper
EV Building, Concordia University
Peel
Metcalfe
Mansfield
McGill College
Robert-Bourassa
Baile
Canadian Centre for Architecture
Guy
Mackay
Bishop
Crescent
René-Lévesque
Square Dorchester
CCA Garden
1250 boulevard René-Lévesque
Place du Canada
Autoroute Ville-Marie
Métro Bonaventure
de la Gauchetière
Métro Georges-Vanier
Métro Lucien-L'Allier
Métro Square-Victoria–OACI
Saint-Antoine
Saint-Jacques
0
200 metres
2 minutes to walk
Notre-Dame

DOWNTOWN

Montrealers not only work in the downtown core – they live, play and shop there. To go downtown invariably means to walk along Ste. Catherine, first fashionable in the 1890s, when department stores moved up the hill from Square Victoria. The newly wealthy had begun to flee the original downtown in Old Montreal in 1860 to build elegant homes to the north of Sherbrooke. The city's financial centre, however, remained on St. Jacques in Old Montreal until Place Ville Marie was built in 1962.

Construction of the metro in 1966 changed the nature of downtown. Underground connections linked buildings not only to the subway system but also to one another; developers started to look for sites contiguous to metro stations. Construction of Place des Arts and Complexe Desjardins – both "hard-wired" to the metro – succeeded in moving the core of downtown slightly to the east.

A 1980s proposal to widen McGill College, the avenue leading north from Place Ville Marie to Sherbrooke, instigated public consultations that were as much about corporate presence in the downtown as they were about street width and setbacks. The granite and glass towers from that period speak to the city's brief flirtation with postmodernism.

Much of 1990s downtown construction was institutional – universities, museums and theatres – and in part government funded. Since 2000, an upswing in the economy has meant a rush to convert existing buildings into condominiums and to erect new ones. While reinforcing the mixed residential and commercial character of Montreal's downtown, the new towers – particularly the cluster on René-Lévesque around the hockey mecca Bell Centre – are a disappointment.

MAISON ALCAN

The integration of new construction with restored or renovated buildings to create Alcan's world headquarters on Sherbrooke was an innovation at the beginning of the 1980s. It marked a turning point in corporate Montreal's attitude towards constructing offices, demonstrating that a tall building is not the only answer to corporate presence in the city. In this case, a new eight-storey pavilion was built behind three 19th-century greystone houses and a 1920s hotel, which were converted into offices; the whole is linked by a glazed atrium. The Davis Building was clad in a beautifully detailed champagne-coloured aluminum curtain wall that is aging effortlessly.

The ensemble of Maison Alcan includes the former Emmanuel Congregational Church and a second office building, originally built for the Salvation Army, creating an urban park that is a reflection of partner-in-charge Ray Affleck's views on the importance of the relationship of inside to outside, of being able to move freely through the building.

The 2015 departure of Rio Tinto Alcan from its Sherbrooke Street headquarters will mean changes for Maison Alcan. It is to be hoped that the next use is as imaginative as the 1983 project.

Architects	**Arcop Associates**
Client	**Alcan Aluminium Ltd.**
Completed	**1983**
Address	**1188 Rue Sherbrooke Ouest**
Métro	**Peel**
Access	**exterior only**

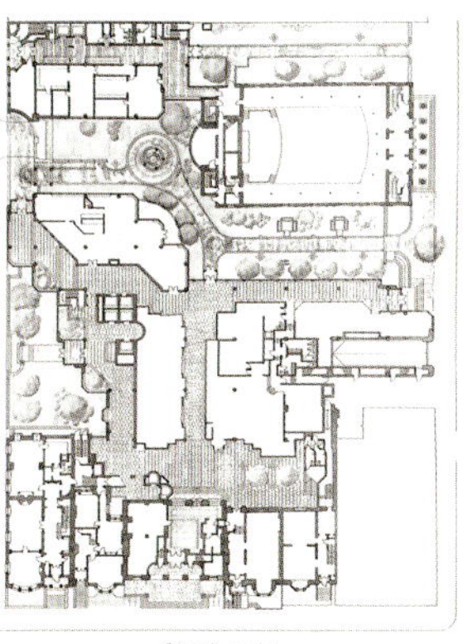
Sherbrooke

MONTREAL MUSEUM OF FINE ARTS

Jean-Noël-Desmarais Pavilion

The Montreal Museum of Fine Arts has built a *cité muséale* anchored by the original 1912 Edward & W.S. Maxwell building on Sherbrooke Street.

The 1991 pavilion, sited directly opposite the original building, was controversial from the very beginning of the project. The original scheme, calling for the demolition of the New Sherbrooke apartment building, excited opposition from many Montrealers and generated public consultations.

The outcome was the decision to retain the shell of the apartment building for museum offices, which added to the list of constraints that the difficult and highly visible site imposed. Safdie's solution was a series of three volumes connected by bridges – an entry pavilion, the refitted New Sherbrooke and a pavilion to the south of the alley running from Bishop to Crescent. The monumentality of the entry, a massive masonry arch opening to an atrium, may have been a deliberate counterpoint to the streetscape but has still never truly looked as if it belonged.

"The Fifth Pavilion"– the Michal and Renata Hornstein Pavilion for Peace – by architects Atelier TAG / JLP will open in 2017 on Bishop, immediately south of the Desmarais pavilion. The architects describe their 2013 competition winner as being clad in a "lacework of limestone." The insertion will provide both galleries and educational spaces.

Architects	**Moshe Safdie / Desnoyers Mercure et Associés / Lemay Leclerc**
Client	**Montreal Museum of Fine Arts**
Completed	**1991**
Address	**1380 Rue Sherbrooke Ouest**
Métro	**Guy-Concordia**
Access	**see website**

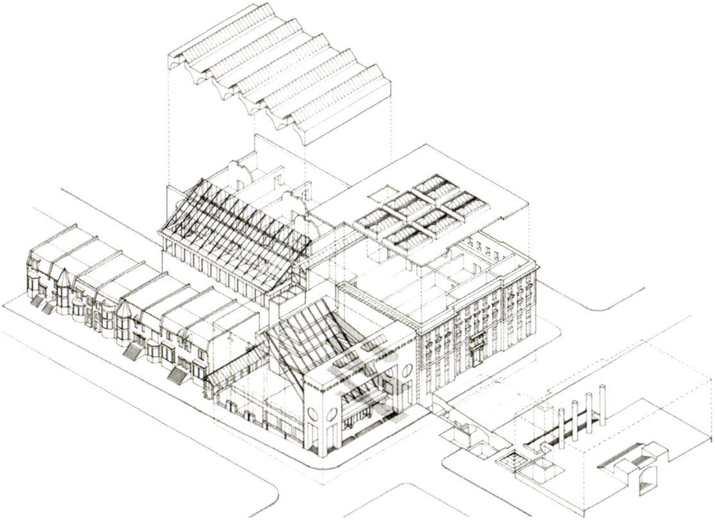

MONTREAL MUSEUM OF FINE ARTS

Claire and Marc Bourgie Pavilion of Quebec and Canadian Art

The 2011 addition to the museum's *cité muséale* reuses the Erskine and American United Church as a concert hall and inserts a marble-clad slice of exhibition galleries behind it, making a strong and respectful statement about being contemporary. While the museum's 2008 acquisition of the 1894 church by A.C. Hutchison seemed entirely fitting, repurposing the building as museum space was problematic, until Pierre Bourgie proposed reusing it as a concert hall and contributed to its realization with the gallery. The conversion of the church is deftly done and conserves the essence of its 1938 interior as redone by architects Nobbs & Hyde, including restoration of eighteen Tiffany windows.

The new pavilion is clad in the same marble as both the original 1912 building and the 1991 Desmarais pavilion on the south side of Sherbrooke. Provencher Roy elected to hang the marble in panels, appearing as they did in the quarry. Six storeys house the collection of Quebec and Canadian art, with the earliest works at the top. The first surprise is the captivating views of the city from the glazed public spaces adjoining the galleries; the second surprise is the tunnel under Sherbrooke Street that links the pavilion to the Desmarais pavilion – an extraordinary space for contemporary art.

On du Musée, the sculpture garden/public space was created by the City of Montreal, reinforcing the museum's campus quality. Closed off at Sherbrooke in the summer months, the street is the site of installations by Montreal landscape architects.

Architects	**Provencher Roy + Associés architectes**
Masonry restoration consultant	**(concert hall) DFS Architecture et design**
Sculpture garden design	**Ville de Montréal, Atelier d'aménagement et de design urbain**
Client	**Montreal Museum of Fine Arts**
Completed	**2011**
Address	**1380 Rue Sherbrooke Ouest (entry to all museum pavilions is via the Desmarais pavilion)**
Métro	**Guy-Concordia**
Access	**see website**

CANADIAN CENTRE FOR ARCHITECTURE

At the same time as it fulfils its mandate as a research centre and museum promoting the art and history of architecture, the Canadian Centre for Architecture also establishes its place clearly as a Montreal building. Its scale and volume reflect both the residential character of its Shaughnessy Village neighbourhood and the institutional nature of the convents within a stone's throw on René-Lévesque.

The CCA was built around the existing 1874 Shaughnessy House; the two wings of the new construction house the study centre to the east and the theatre to the west; exhibition galleries are in the central core. The collection of prints, drawings, photos, books and other objects is stored in two floors of vaults below grade. The symmetry of the construction is generated by the party wall between the two halves of the original semi-detached house, visible on the north entry façade as a deftly incised expansion joint.

The choice of limestone – the stone out of which much of Montreal is built – for the exterior walls, and Quebec granite, aluminum and maple for the interior was a deliberate decision that reflects the CCA's sense of place. Designed to last a hundred years, the construction of the building demonstrates a commitment to quality that is *sans pareil*.

Architects	**Peter Rose**
Consulting architect	**Phyllis Lambert**
Associate architect	**Erol Argun**
Client	**Canadian Centre for Architecture**
Completed	**1989**
Address	**1920 Rue Baile**
Métro	**Guy-Concordia**
Access	**see website**

CCA GARDEN

The demolition in the mid-20th century of the Victorian-era houses on the south side of René-Lévesque and the construction of access ramps to the Ville-Marie expressway created a curious vestigial piece of land directly across the street from the Canadian Centre for Architecture. Charney's 1988 competition-winning design makes full use of the spectacular position of the land at the edge of the escarpment. It uses the rich history of the area to create layers and meaning in every aspect of the garden, making it a place of discovery.

The arcade evokes the demolished houses and mirrors the 1874 Shaughnessy House; the sculpture court is lined with allegorical columns that refer to the history of architecture and draw the eye to the cityscape below the belvedere. Low walls are sited on the cadastral lines that determined Montreal's street grid.

An apple orchard on the eastern edge of the garden recalls the original use of this part of the city – all the vegetation is deliberately indigenous. The CCA Garden serves as a place of reflection and respite in an area of the city that desperately lacked breathing space.

Architects	**Melvin Charney**
Landscape architect	**Gerrard and Mackars**
Client	**Canadian Centre for Architecture**
Completed	**1989**
Address	**Boul. René-Lévesque between du Fort and Saint-Marc**
Métro	**Guy-Concordia**
Access	**public**

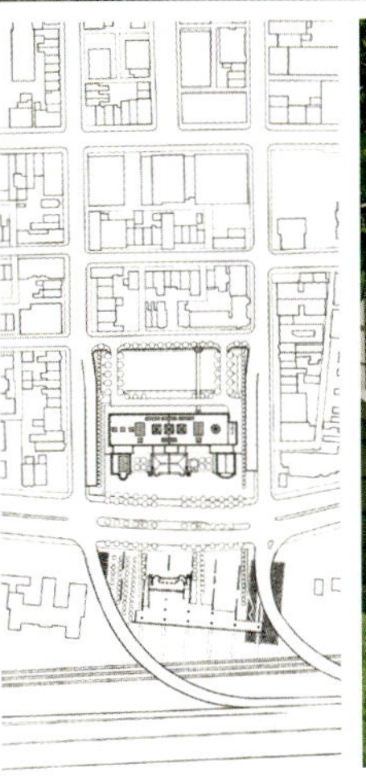

EV BUILDING, CONCORDIA UNIVERSITY

Concordia University's downtown campus is made of concrete streets and sidewalks; there is little open land, and sites available for new construction are constrained. The architects' solution for a new building to house Engineering/Computer Science and Visual Arts was what they describe as "stacked academic neighbourhoods." The complex comprises two pavilions connected horizontally by intersecting circulation systems. Vertically, each pavilion has a series of stacked atria with circular stairs linking different floors and terraces.

For a university building, it has a very corporate look, with its projecting canopies at roof level and banded curtain wall. (The exception is the photographic floral mural by Nicolas Baier splashed over the east façade.) Much has been made of the transparency at the concourse level, but the three-storey interior space it reveals at the main entry corner at Guy and Ste. Catherine is rather unresolved. By contrast, the connections to below grade are some of the most interesting parts of the building: the escalator that leads to the metro station slices dramatically down into the underground level beside an illuminated wall.

Its sibling-building, the John Molson School of Business, also designed by KPMB, is across the street on a tight corner site at Guy and de Maisonneuve. Completed in 2009, it uses the same language and pushes the interconnectedness further, with gathering spaces linked to atria and circulation.

Architects	**Kuwabara Payne McKenna Blumberg / Fichten Soiferman et Associés**
Client	**Concordia University**
Completed	**2005**
Address	**1515 Rue Sainte-Catherine Ouest**
Métro	**Guy-Concordia**
Access	**university hours**

1250 BOULEVARD RENÉ-LÉVESQUE

There were many tall buildings built in Montreal's downtown core in the 1980s, but the only one that comes close to the quality of its predecessors from the 1960s – Place Ville Marie, CIBC and Westmount Square – is 1250 René-Levesque (known to many Montrealers as the IBM Building for its original anchor tenant). Viewed from a distance, it is a classic skyscraper, with a base, a shaft and the grand gesture of a giant beak-like cap reaching towards the river. A closer view reveals the curve of the principal façade and the cluster of pavilions around the base. The volumes are deliberately complex. Black granite, white granite, aluminum and glass are played against one another.

Sitting strategically just west of Square Dorchester and north of Windsor Station, the building has volumetrically well-developed relationships with its neighbours. The changes of level and scale make the plaza more interesting than most, despite the chilly black granite pergola on Stanley.

Since 2012, no fewer than eight new towers – six condominiums, a hotel and an office building – have been built in the sector immediately to the west of 1250 René-Lévesque. While an argument can be made for building towers in this area, the design of the buildings is uniformly disappointing.

Architects	**Kohn Pedersen Fox / Larose Petrucci et Associés**
Client	**IBM Canada / La Société immobilière Marathon, Limitée**
Completed	**1993**
Address	**1250 Boul. René-Lévesque**
Métro	**Bonaventure**
Access	**atrium open weekdays during office hours**

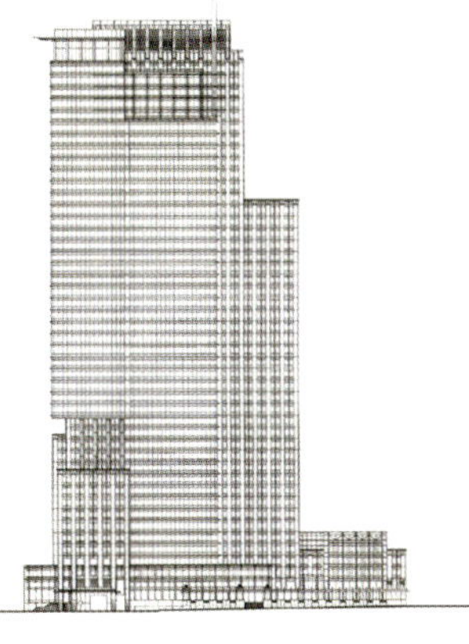

SQUARE DORCHESTER AND PLACE DU CANADA

Square Dorchester, rebuilt in 2010, and Place du Canada, rebuilt in 2015, form one of Montreal's great public spaces. Designed with a subtlety and a sureness of hand, they give people walking through them a sense of absolute rightness. Both had become seriously dilapidated in the latter part of the 20th century, betraying their elegant Victorian origins. The reconstruction is faithful in intent to the original plan – formal symmetry in Square Dorchester, the picturesque in Place du Canada.

Square Dorchester is a significant commemorative space, with the monument to the Boer War, "Strathcona's Horse," at its centre. Granite pathways traverse gently sloped grass mounds, benches are generously sited along them and the whole is well lit. People working in surrounding office buildings eat lunch in the square, with a view to the Sun Life Building, Mary, Queen of the World Cathedral and the 1962 CIBC Building – a tissue sample of Montreal's history as a city.

But the most fascinating aspect of what could be seen as Montreal's great urban room is what one doesn't see, the only clue being Claude Cormier's cross-shaped icons inset into the granite walkways. From 1799 to 1855, the area was Montreal's principal Catholic cemetery, expropriated by the City in 1872 to create a square when the Saint-Antoine Cemetery was relocated to the northern slopes of Mount Royal.

Architects	**Groupe Cardinal Hardy / Claude Cormier et associés, architectes paysagistes**
Client	**Ville de Montréal**
Completed	**Square Dorchester 2010, Place du Canada 2015**
Address	**Boul. René-Lévesque between Rue Peel and Rue Metcalfe**
Métro	**Peel**
Access	**public**

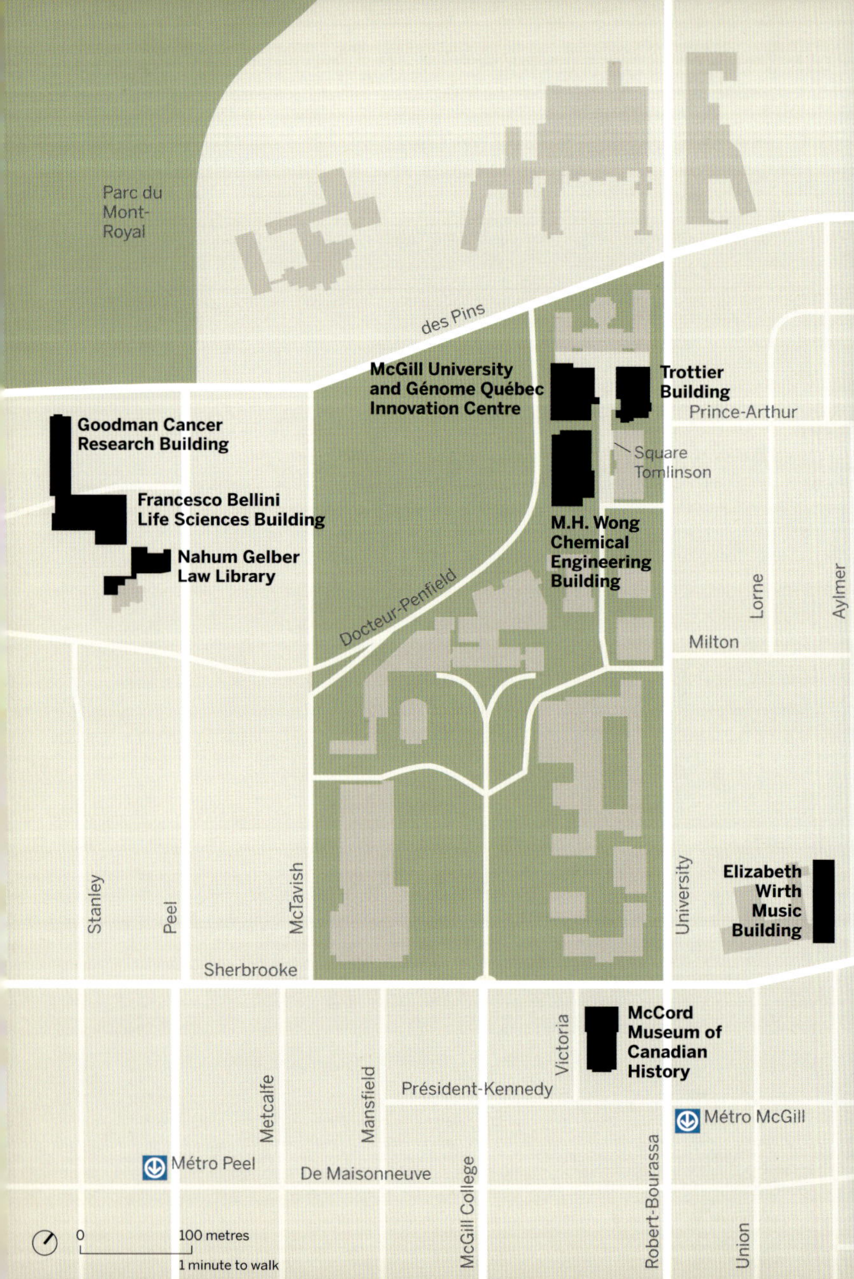
Parc du Mont-Royal
des Pins
McGill University and Génome Québec Innovation Centre
Trottier Building
Prince-Arthur
Goodman Cancer Research Building
Square Tomlinson
Francesco Bellini Life Sciences Building
M.H. Wong Chemical Engineering Building
Nahum Gelber Law Library
Docteur-Penfield
Lorne
Aylmer
Milton
Elizabeth Wirth Music Building
Stanley
Peel
McTavish
University
Sherbrooke
McCord Museum of Canadian History
Victoria
Président-Kennedy
Metcalfe
Mansfield
Métro McGill
Métro Peel
De Maisonneuve
McGill College
Robert-Bourassa
Union
0
100 metres
1 minute to walk

McGILL UNIVERSITY

The main campus of McGill University is the site of James McGill's country estate, which was left in 1813 as a legacy, along with £10,000, to establish the university. Philanthropists such as Sir William Macdonald underwrote the construction of much of the campus in the latter half of the 19th century – a period of expansion that continued until the 1920s. Post-1945 construction started to encroach on the green space and produced mixed results architecturally as the university built rapidly to accommodate the baby boom.

Like the three other Montreal universities, McGill went on a building spree starting in the late 1990s with a half dozen different new buildings inserted into the campus. The McGill neighbourhood is actually much larger than the main campus, having spread into the late-Victorian mansions on the slopes of the mountain. The challenge for the university is how to maintain an ensemble of significant buildings that runs the gamut from 19th-century houses to modernist towers while continuously adapting them to meet their needs.

M.H. WONG CHEMICAL ENGINEERING BUILDING

The 1998 M.H. Wong Building was the first new construction on the McGill University campus in twenty years. Inserted into the northeast corner of the downtown campus, it encompasses the 1948 Foster Cyclotron Building and houses departments that were bursting out of the McConnell Engineering Building to the south.

The structure has two distinct faces: a glass and aluminum curtain wall on Docteur-Penfield, the city side, and a limestone façade on the campus side. Materials allude to the 19th-century buildings that dominate the campus; the two-storey metallurgical foundry is clad in lead-covered copper. The north façade, the most interesting volumetrically, is now obscured in part by the 2003 construction of the Genome Building.

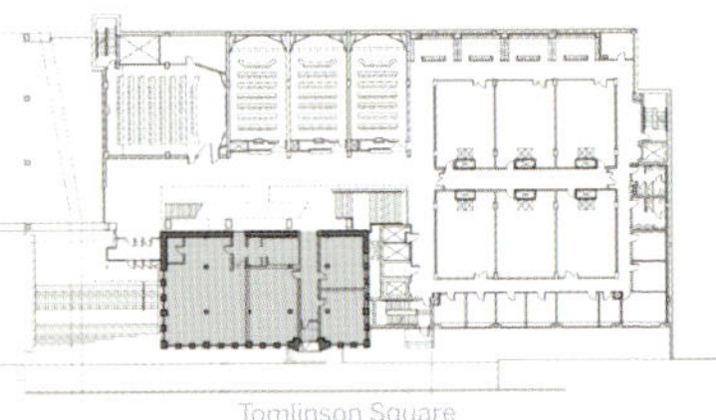

Architects	**Jodoin Lamarre Pratte et Associés / Marosi + Troy**
Client	**McGill University**
Completed	**1998**
Address	**3610 Rue University**
Métro	**McGill**
Access	**university hours**

TROTTIER BUILDING

In contrast to the cool sobriety of the Genome Building, the Trottier Building is characterized by an openness and a sense of being an extension of the landscape of Place Tomlinson. Like the Genome and Wong buildings, the Trottier Building is double sided – it addresses the interior campus space on the west and University Street on the east. The restrained stone-and-glass east façade has been skilfully added to the streetscape.

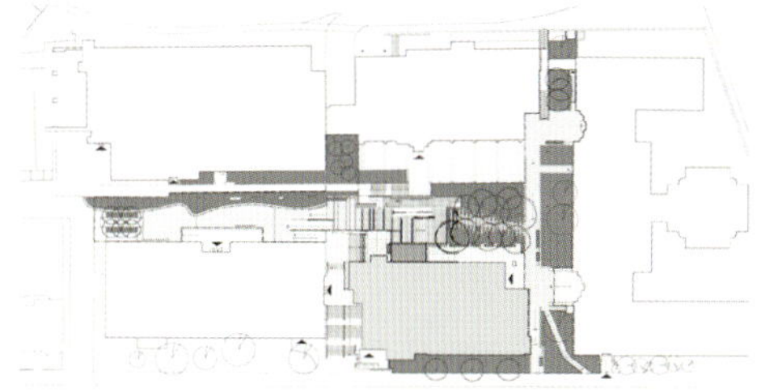

Architects	**Marosi + Troy / Jodoin Lamarre Pratte et Associés**
Client	**McGill University**
Completed	**2004**
Address	**3630 Rue University**
Métro	**McGill**
Access	**university hours**

McGILL UNIVERSITY AND GÉNOME QUÉBEC INNOVATION CENTRE

"Legible" is the word that best describes the Genome Building, as it is known. One sees immediately how to move through the building – all the more remarkable given that it has two fronts, one on the west towards Docteur-Penfield and one on the east towards Tomlinson Square.

Offices for researchers are on the more public west façade. Each office is articulated and canted slightly towards Mount Royal, protected by a screen of metal grid against the sun. Laboratories are on the sombre east façade on the campus side, behind a more formal curtain wall that sits on a limestone base. The two functions of the building are knit together by a three-storey vertical atrium, with circulation through it and conference rooms looking onto it. Common areas provide places for both formal and informal meetings.

Architects	**Kuwabara Payne McKenna Blumberg / Fichten Soiferman et Associés**
Client	**McGill University**
Completed	**2003**
Address	**740 Av. du Docteur-Penfield, enter via Milton**
Métro	**McGill**
Access	**interior lobbies only – university hours**

FRANCESCO BELLINI LIFE SCIENCES BUILDING AND GOODMAN CANCER RESEARCH BUILDING

The site is a mass of constraints: on the slopes of the historic and natural site of Mount Royal, a very narrow and steeply sloped site, with Square Mile houses to the east, two existing 1960s McGill medical buildings and an existing underground parking garage. The two research buildings respond to these constraints in a remarkably coherent fashion, linking the McIntyre Medical and Stewart Biological Sciences buildings and connecting a concentrated mass of laboratories to form the Life Sciences Complex.

The cancer research pavilion runs north-south, seven storeys high where it connects to the Bellini pavilion and three where it opens very neatly onto des Pins. Its green roof is visible from the slope of the mountain. At right angles to the cancer research pavilion, the L-shaped life sciences building slides along the east-west laneway from Peel to Sir-William-Osler. A four-storey wood-slatted atrium provides a quasi-public space.

Glass not only serves to define the juxtaposition with the existing buildings, it also creates labs and offices with an abundance of daylight. Curiously, this also means that from the outside, everybody's office clutter is easy to see among the lab equipment!

Architects	**Diamond Schmitt / Provencher Roy**
Client	**McGill University**
Completed	**2008**
Address	**3649 Promenade Sir-William-Osler**
Métro	**Peel**
Access	**exterior only**

NAHUM GELBER LAW LIBRARY

Old Chancellor Day Hall, the 1892 Square Mile mansion by the American architect Bruce Price, is the core of a cluster of buildings that are home to McGill's Faculty of Law. The Nahum Gelber Library was added at right angles to Chancellor Day Hall, sited so as to create an entry courtyard which sets up an opposition to the urban language of the surrounding area.

The choice of materials – brown brick and red stone – reflects the Victorian houses on Peel, while the rectangular box volume has more to do with the library's function as container. The two-storey triangular window, clearly intended to echo the surrounding turrets, is an example of the wit that infuses all of Hanganu's buildings.

The relationship of inside to outside and the presence of natural light play an important role; as one enters the lobby, a two-storey-high window reveals a small garden carved into the face of the hill behind the building, and slit-like windows mark the locations of study carrels.

Playfulness with industrial materials – another Hanganu trademark – is evident throughout: a purple metal spiral stair curves upward to the reference area, where the reading room occupies the top floors, and floor grates are used on the entrance doors.

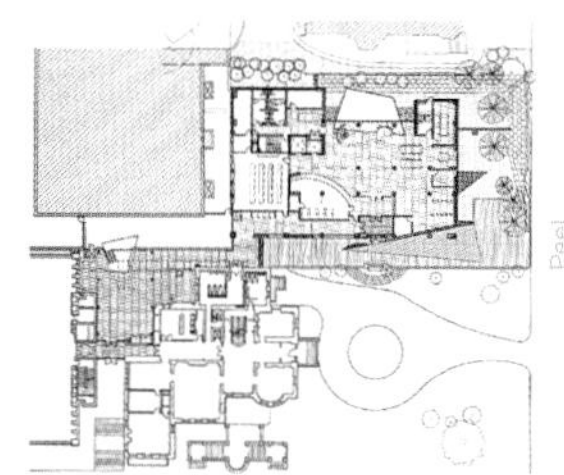

Architects	**Dan S. Hanganu**
Client	**McGill University**
Completed	**1998**
Address	**3660 Rue Peel**
Métro	**Peel**
Access	**interior – library lobby only, library hours**

McCORD MUSEUM OF CANADIAN HISTORY

The McCord Museum has been housed in the former McGill Student Union since 1967, when the original 1906 Percy Nobbs building was gutted to accommodate David Ross McCord's extensive collection of artefacts of Canadian history.

In the late 1980s, a donation by the J.W. McConnell Foundation finally allowed the museum to build both exhibition space and climate-controlled storage. The programme included both renovation of the existing building and new construction that tripled the existing floor area by extending the building to the south. Clad in the same limestone as the original building, the extension speaks a language that is both respectful and elegant in its own right. The glazed link and a lightwell onto an interior courtyard to the east mark the passage from old to new construction; large galleries are housed in the addition, smaller galleries for the permanent collections, main entrance, boutique and café in the original structure. A carefully controlled palette of materials, including slate, is used consistently through the building.

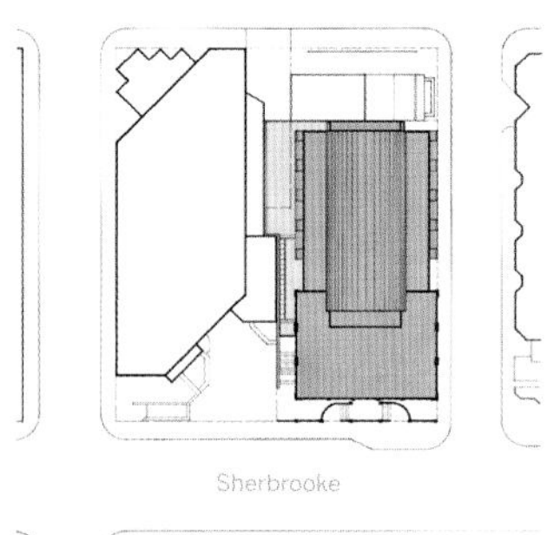

Architects	**Jodoin Lamarre Pratte et Associés / LeMoyne Lapointe Magne**
Client	**McCord Museum of Canadian History**
Completed	**1991**
Address	**696 Rue Sherbrooke Ouest**
Métro	**McGill**
Access	**see website**

ELIZABETH WIRTH MUSIC BUILDING

The Elizabeth Wirth Music Building demands attention, sitting as it does where Sherbrooke curves slightly at the corner of Aylmer. Juxtaposed and linked to the 1899 Strathcona Hall building (originally Royal Victoria College) housing McGill's Schulich School of Music, it anchors the southeast corner of the McGill campus. The original programme to house the music library was expanded to include a five-storey-high scoring stage, rehearsal spaces, a two-hundred-seat recital hall and an opera studio. On a relatively narrow site, fitting in all of this meant assembling a three-dimensional puzzle, then literally digging three storeys down into the rock of Mount Royal to make room for it.

There is a controlled complexity to the building's façades – on the eastern side, the limestone base and horizontal bands of grey zinc represent the "geological" presence of the massive sound studio, and the library, office and rehearsal spaces above it. By contrast, the western façade is rusting steel topped by black glass, fragmented by contrasting slits.

The three-storey library sits behind a glazed slot on the front façade, creating a window-on-the-world place to sit and work. Wonderful small spaces and junctions happen all through the building, an attitude that characterizes Saucier + Perrotte's work.

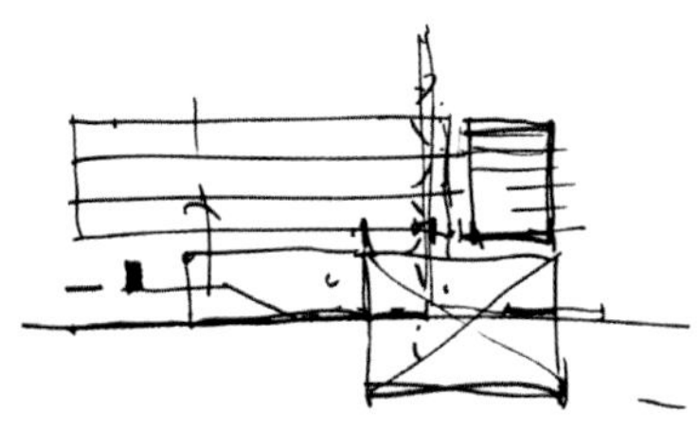

Architects	**Saucier + Perrotte / Menkès Shooner Dagenais LeTourneux**
Client	**McGill University**
Completed	**2005**
Address	**527 Rue Sherbrooke Ouest**
Métro	**McGill**
Access	**university hours**

Four Points

Milton
Durocher
Hutchison
du Parc
Jeanne-Mance
Sainte-Famille
Saint-Urbain
Quartier des spectacles
Sherbrooke
Complexe des Sciences de l'UQÀM
Clark
Saint-Laurent
Saint-Dominique
De Bullion
de l'Hôtel-de-Ville
Ontario
Sanguinet
Saint-Denis
Berri
Saint-Hubert
Maison symphonique de Montréal
Promenade des Artistes
Ontario
Parterre
Métro Place-des-Arts
De Maisonneuve
De Maisonneuve
City Councillors
Place des Festivals
Mayor
Métro Saint-Laurent
Place Émilie-Gamelin
Esplanade
Place des Arts
Métro Berri-UQAM
Sainte-Catherine
Maison du développement durable
René-Lévesque
0
100 metres
1 minute to walk

QUARTIER DES SPECTACLES

The Quartier des Spectacles is the second deliberately created neighbourhood in Montreal, following on the heels of the 2004 Quartier international de Montréal. Within its one-square-kilometre area, it groups together private and public performance venues with new public spaces and a unifying graphic language.

In the 18th century, this part of the city was the Faubourg Saint-Laurent, a rural area outside the fortified city stretching across St. Laurent Blvd., which ran towards the north. At the beginning of the 19th century, the walls were demolished and the quartier densified with the construction of institutions like Saint Patrick's Church, and then industries. St. Laurent ("The Main") was the principal commercial street, a glorious riot of stores with housing above that became home to the waves of immigrants who arrived in the city starting at the beginning of the 20th century.

The 1963 concert hall complex project, Place des Arts, changed the character and nature of the area, but it was the Jazz Festival's informal use of the plaza in the 1980s that pushed the neighbourhood towards its current vocation.

The Quartier des Spectacles partnership was formed by twenty "stakeholder members" (theatres, clubs and concert venues) in 2003, and initially development was limited to supporting outdoor events. In 2007, all levels of government committed to a significant program of construction of new public spaces and infrastructure focused on the Place des Arts "pole," which was expanded in 2012 following public consultations to include a section of the Quartier Latin, enlarging the *quartier* farther to the east.

QUARTIER DES SPECTACLES

Can you make a *quartier*? The idea for contriving the *quartier* in the first place was to link existing performance spaces and venues, to make a place out of what were at best tenuous connections between buildings with the same use.

Daoust Lestage – the architects and urban designers responsible for the Quartier international de Montréal – were commissioned to develop a master plan and design for the new *quartier*. Four phases of construction started with the public spaces, most notably the large-scale Place des Festivals, followed by the Promenade des artistes and the Parterre.

The subtlest element in the making of the *quartier* is the pedestrianizing of a stretch of Ste. Catherine every summer, made possible by a continuous surface of granite pavers across street and sidewalk. Bollards separate the two zones in the winter.

In 2012, the Quartier des Spectacles' stakeholders proposed extending the neighbourhood to include the Quartier Latin to the east of the Place des Arts/St. Laurent sector including reactivating spaces like Place Emilie-Gamelin with the imaginative Jardins Gamelin in 2015.

The critique that has been lobbed most often at the Quartier des Spectacles is that it is an exercise in branding – witness the graphic signature, web design and signage that have been a coherent whole since the *quartier*'s inception. With time, however, perhaps the neigbourhood is growing into the image its branding created.

Is it a success? If successfully serving as the festival headquarters for a city that defines itself by its festivals is a measure of success, yes; if attracting other projects (no fewer than forty-eight) is a measure, certainly.

Architects	**Daoust Lestage Inc.**
Client	**Ville de Montréal**
Completed	**2009 phase 1 / 2016 phase 2**
Address	**from Rue City Councillors to Rue Saint-Hubert, from René-Lévesque to Sherbrooke**
Métro	**Place-des-Arts / Saint-Laurent / Berri-UQAM**
Access	**public**

PLACE DES FESTIVALS

Designing a new public space that can comfortably accommodate tens of thousands of people for a Jazz Festival concert and that can also look inviting on an early spring afternoon with only a few brave people seeking sun is no small challenge. The signature space of the Quartier des Spectacles proclaims its large-scale use very clearly – four angled lighting masts lean over the hard surface and tiers of bleacher-like granite steps climb up the slope on the western edge. However, it's the smaller gestures that make it interesting: fountains installed at grade spray mist or spout water; urban furniture is smartly detailed.

Elegant aluminum/glass-box restaurants that seat sixty people each, the two Vitrines habitées on the Jeanne-Mance side help mitigate the presence of loading dock doors for the Musée d'art contemporain on the east side of the Place des Festivals. It's worth remembering that this new public space was created out of squibs of vacant land and inserted into a landscape dominated by the concrete institutions of Place des Arts and the museum. As other elements of the Quartier des Spectacles have been built, including linked public spaces like the Promenade des Artistes along de Maisonneuve, the Place des Festivals has begun to sit more comfortably. On the west side, the Maison du Festival Rio Tinto Alcan, the transformation of the Wilder building to house Les Grands Ballets Canadiens and the construction of the new Ïlot Balmoral for the National Film Board of Canada give life and substance to this public space.

Architects and urban designers	**Daoust Lestage Inc. (also architects of the Vitrines habitées, 2010)**
Client	**Ville de Montréal**
Completed	**2009**
Address	**Rue Jeanne-Mance from Sainte-Catherine to de Maisonneuve**
Métro	**Place-des-Arts**
Access	**public**

COMPLEXE DES SCIENCES DE L'UQÀM

Montreal's four universities went on a building spree in the late 1990s – UQÀM (Université du Québec à Montréal) went so far as to construct a whole precinct for its science buildings. In 1997, on a mostly vacant block, Saia Barbarese was responsible for the first project – the elliptical Pavillon Président-Kennedy – along with the restoration of the 1917 École Technique at the corner of Jeanne-Mance and Sherbrooke.

The campus was completed in 2005 by the construction of a series of buildings and a coherent web of paths and public spaces. Saia Barbarese Topouzanov conceived the ensemble of pavilions to house classrooms, laboratories, research areas, student residences and the "Cœur des sciences," a former forge used by École Technique students now converted to a public meeting space. All the pavilions are built in the yellow brick characteristic of early-20th-century Montreal institutions. The use of coloured glass throughout produces fascinating plays of light – least successful perhaps in the most visible pavilion on Sherbrooke.

The act of walking through the campus from Sherbrooke to Président-Kennedy gives one a sense of containment, of being set apart in an enclosed world, only to emerge onto the northern edge of the bustling Quartier des Spectacles.

Architects	**Saia Barbarese Topouzanov / Tétreault Parent Langued**
Landscape architect	**Claude Cormier**
Client	**Université du Québec à Montréal**
Completed	**2005**
Address	**200 Rue Sherbrooke Ouest (Pavillon Sherbrooke);** **141 Av. du Président-Kennedy (Sciences biologiques)**
Métro	**Place-des-Arts**
Access	**university hours**

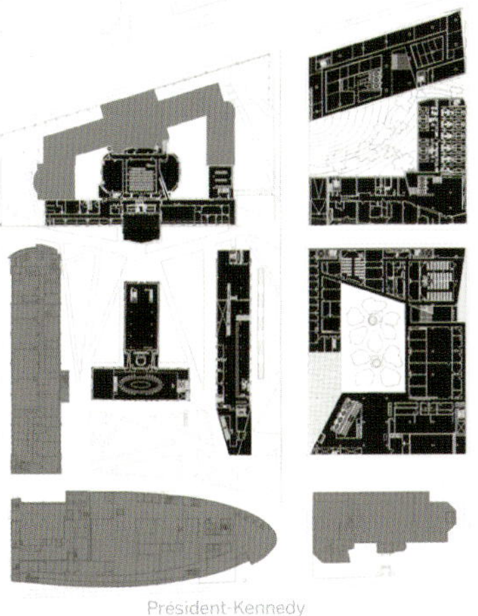
Président-Kennedy

PLACE DES ARTS AND MAISON SYMPHONIQUE DE MONTRÉAL

Place des Arts was a 1963 project propelled by Mayor Jean Drapeau with the specific intent of creating a cultural axis in the eastern part of downtown Montreal. The site plan and the monumental colonnaded structure, the Salle Wilfrid-Pelletier, were designed by the young architectural firm of Affleck, Desbarats, Dimakopoulos, Lebensold, Michaud and Sise. The plaza was further defined by the addition of two smaller theatres on the east side in 1967 and the construction of the Musée d'art contemporain in 1992.

The final piece of the puzzle was the Maison symphonique de Montréal, conceived specifically as a concert hall for the Montreal Symphony Orchestra. Much anticipated – many different sites having been considered over the previous twenty-five years – the new shoebox-shaped hall was slid into the northeast corner of the site. The concert hall opened in 2011, before the exterior was completed and the warm beechwood room proved to be acoustically as beautiful as the hall. Sadly, when the exterior was revealed, there was an overwhelming sense of missed opportunity, as the materials, the fenestration and the entry all seemed more ordinary than they should have been. A case of the private-public partnership process getting in the way of good design.

The plaza has been reconfigured many times – driven at least in part by its use as a platform for multiple festivals. Now a public space that is a part of the larger entity of Quartier des Spectacles, the plaza is to be redesigned by Provencher Roy in time for Montreal's 375th anniversary celebrations in 2017.

Architects	**Diamond Schmitt + Aedifica**
Client	**Ministère de la culture et des communications**
Completed	**2012**
Address	**1600 Rue Saint-Urbain**
Métro	**Place-des-Arts**
Access	**exterior only**

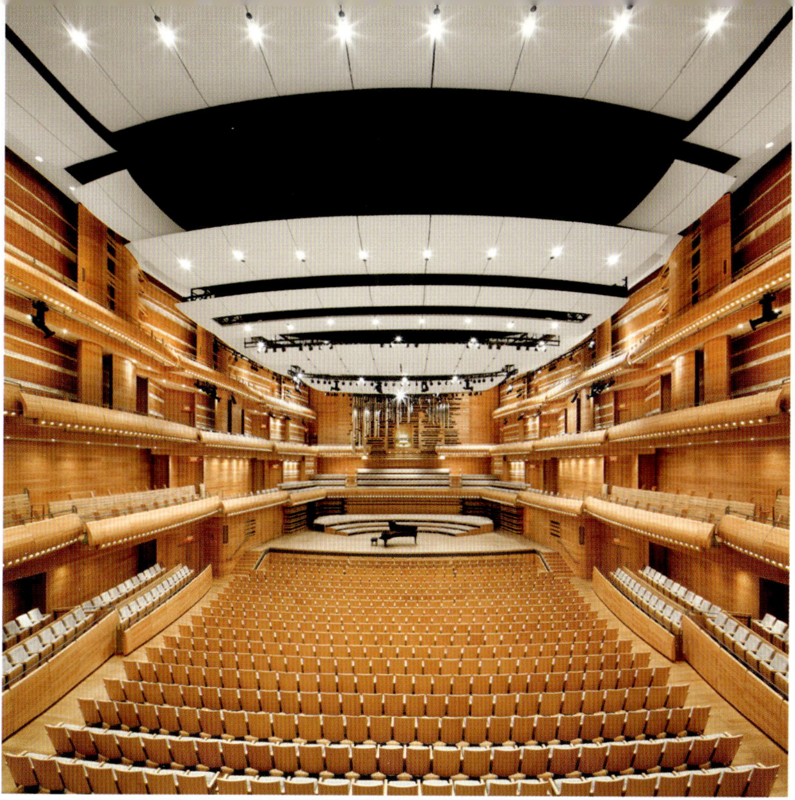

MAISON DU DÉVELOPPEMENT DURABLE

The first thing that strikes the passerby about the Maison du développement durable is how comfortably it sits on the corner of Ste. Catherine and Clark. An accessible, open to the public space/garden that is an integral part of the project, it looks as if it should be there. This is all the more interesting when one learns that the building is dedicated to sustainable development and houses a cluster of community organizations and a daycare. The choice of site in the downtown core clearly is part of the message that densification is viable and that it's not necessary to build parking spaces except for bikes.

Achieving good design while meeting the requirements for LEED Platinum certification is demanding. Here the simplicity of the materials used is an expression of the architects' intention to minimize – which also meets the certification criteria. Some elements are exuberant rather than minimal, like the living wall and the Parc Hydro-Québec with its thirty mature trees. The metal grid of the park abutting Théâtre du Nouveau Monde is an abstraction of transmission towers!

Architects	**Menkès Shooner Dagenais LeTourneux**
Landscape architect	**Claude Cormier**
Client	**Maison du développement durable / Equiterre**
Completed	**2011**
Address	**50 Rue Sainte-Catherine Ouest**
Métro	**Saint-Laurent**
Access	**lobby only**

MAISON DU
DÉVELOPPEMENT DURABLE

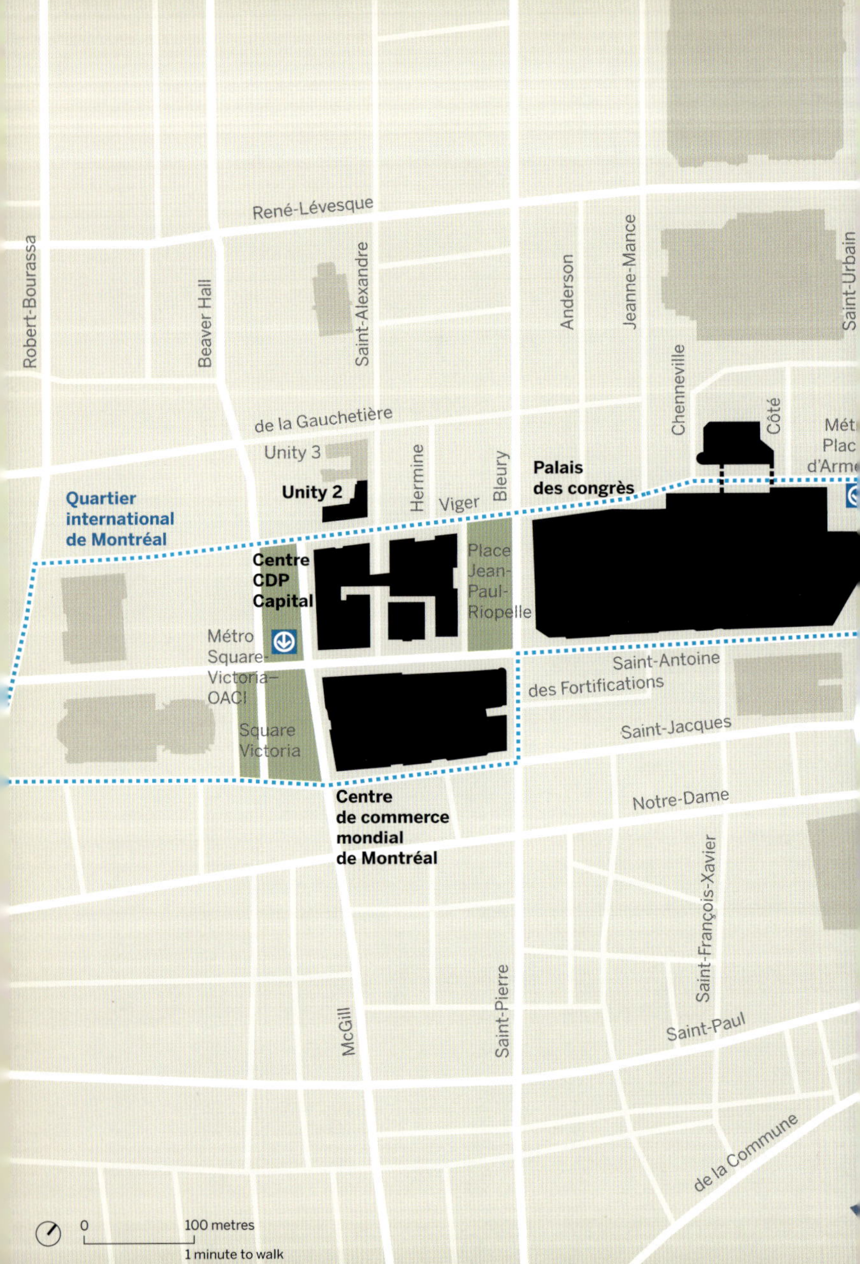
René-Lévesque
Robert-Bourassa
Beaver Hall
Saint-Alexandre
Anderson
Jeanne-Mance
Saint-Urbain
Chenneville
Côté
de la Gauchetière
Unity 3
Unity 2
Hermine
Viger
Bleury
Palais
des congrès
Quartier
international
de Montréal
Centre
CDP
Capital
Place
Jean-
Paul-
Riopelle
Métro
Square-
Victoria–
OACI
Saint-Antoine
des Fortifications
Saint-Jacques
Square
Victoria
Centre
de commerce
mondial
de Montréal
Notre-Dame
Saint-François-Xavier
McGill
Saint-Pierre
Saint-Paul
de la Commune
0
100 metres
1 minute to walk

QUARTIER INTERNATIONAL DE MONTRÉAL

The Quartier international de Montréal is a "made-to-measure" *quartier*, a 27-hectare neighbourhood created by the owners of the buildings that sit within its borders, in a private-public partnership with three levels of government. It is a massive infrastructure project and arguably the most successful urban-scale intervention in contemporary Montreal.

The area was originally Faubourg Saint-Laurent, a residential suburb to the walled city in the early 19th century and industrialized by the end of the century. Publishing and printing dominated – the strip between St. Alexandre and Bleury, from René-Lévesque south to St. Antoine was known as Paper Hill. Square Victoria, elegant in the 19th century, had deteriorated by the 1950s, and the 1964 construction of the Tour de la Bourse changed its scale forever.

Excavation for the subway system, completed in 1966, and construction of the Ville-Marie expressway in 1974 ripped apart the Faubourg Saint-Laurent. The 1983 construction of the Palais des congrès on top of the depressed expressway only served to further isolate the no-man's land it had created. A 1988 charrette and the 1990 *Cité internationale* competition sought ideas as to how to redevelop the area between University and Bleury, from Viger to St. Antoine. Construction of the Centre de commerce mondial de Montréal, completed in 1991, was the first step to revitalization.

The real spur to action was the 1997 government decision to enlarge the Palais des congrès. Property owners, led by the Caisse de dépôt et placement du Québec and in partnership with all levels of government, seized the opportunity to build over the open trench of the expressway at the same time. In so doing, they created new public space and reconnected the *quartier* to the downtown core and to Old Montreal, an intriguing example of what the builders describe as "participation of the private sector in a project dedicated solely to the improvement of the public domain."

QIM (QUARTIER INTERNATIONAL DE MONTRÉAL)

Place Riopelle is the heart of the Quartier international de Montréal, a public square created by building over the open expressway trench and by appropriating vast areas of parking. A subtle curved line in the hard landscaping of the square is the only clue to the presence of the highway and metro tunnels below. The Centre CDP Capital and the Palais des congrès consciously define the boundaries of this urban room. Trees have been generously planted; Jean-Paul Riopelle's 1969 *La Joute* has been installed surrounded by a fountain.

The other significant intervention in public space is Square Victoria – its original boundaries were restored by rerouting a major city street. Its elegant linear design echoes the formality of the first square, built in 1860 – a long sliver of fountain runs down to the urban forest planted in the southern section.

QIM's network of generously sized, granite-curbed sidewalks and designer Michel Dallaire's street furniture together establish a language for the *quartier* that sets it apart from its neighbours – Old Montreal to the south and the downtown core to the north. A line of limestone-clad columns on Robert-Bourassa creates a new portal to the city. Less apparent but equally important is what you don't see: underground parking, the *RESO* corridors linking buildings to each other and to the metro. QIM is characterized by an attention to detail and a quality of execution that are rare indeed.

Architects	**Daoust Lestage Inc. / Provencher Roy et Associés**
Concept	**Daoust Lestage Inc.**
Client	**Société Quartier international de Montréal**
Completed	**2004**
Address	**from Av. Viger to Rue Saint-Antoine, between Bleury and Robert-Bourassa**
Métro	**Square-Victoria–OACI or Place-d'Armes**
Access	**public**

CENTRE DE COMMERCE MONDIAL DE MONTRÉAL

When one stands on the sidewalk on St. Jacques looking at the façade of the Centre de commerce mondial de Montréal, the scale of this substantial intervention is not immediately apparent – and that is one of the great successes of this 116,000-square-metre project completed in 1991. The developer's concept was to create a horizontal skyscraper by integrating different buildings: the façades of four 19th-century buildings on St. Jacques and one on St. Antoine were retained, while a new structure was built behind. The original lane between the buildings, the Ruelle des fortifications, was glazed over to make an interior street.

In 2004, when the Quartier international de Montréal was created, the original intent of the Centre de commerce mondial, to mediate between old and new, and to generate an international precinct, was finally realized. As part of the Quartier international de Montréal, the Passage St. Pierre was added in 2004. Designed by architects Provencher Roy et associés, it gives access to *RESO*, the underground pedestrian network.

Architects	**Arcop Associates / Provencher Roy et Associés / Gersovitz Becker Moss**
Client	**Sociéte de promotion du Centre de commerce mondial de Montréal**
Completed	**1991**
Address	**747 Rue Square-Victoria**
Métro	**Square-Victoria–OACI or Place-d'Armes**
Access	**atrium open to the public**

PALAIS DES CONGRÈS

In 1999, after a competition fraught with difficulties, the commission to double the existing 92,000-square-metre area of Montreal's convention centre was awarded to the architectural consortium led by Mario Saia. The technically very complex project, which covers an expressway, connects to a metro station and integrates a block of existing buildings, retained the original 1983 Victor Prus building. The architects' response to a demanding programme was to have each façade reflect the character of its individual street, the most controversial of which has been the coloured-glass west wall facing Place Riopelle. The St. Antoine façade, where the new construction subsumed a series of 19th-century buildings, is unfortunate, as it strips the existing structures of their character.

The interior of the Palais des congrès includes a three-hundred-metre-long tapered "street" running from Place Riopelle to St. Urbain. The north-south corridors that lead from this main street to St. Antoine are important, as they connect the convention centre to the urban fabric, including Old Montreal to the south. The vast public space of the hall is fringed by Claude Cormier's *Lipstick Forest* and illuminated by fantastic lozenges of light that stream through the multicoloured façade.

Architects	**Saia Barbarese Topouzanov / Tétrault Parent Languedoc / Aedifica**
Independent architectural consultant	**Hal Ingberg**
Landscape architect	**Claude Cormier**
Client	**Société du Palais des Congrès**
Completed	**2003**
Address	**1001 Place Jean-Paul Riopelle**
Métro	**Place-d'Armes**
Access	**public**

CENTRE CDP CAPITAL

Built on massive 30-by-5.4-metre bridge-like steel beams, the headquarters for the Caisse de dépôt et placement du Québec spans the Ville-Marie expressway below it. An integral part of the Quartier international de Montréal, the building is a deliberate gesture to the city on the part of the agency responsible for investing Quebec's pension funds.

The 70,000-square-metre structure, described by its architects as a horizontal skyscraper, links Place Riopelle to the east and Square Victoria to the west via *Le Parquet*, a nine-storey glazed atrium that bridges St. Alexandre. Projecting into the atrium at the sixth and seventh floors is the 560-square-metre trading pod. The new construction wraps itself around three existing buildings, including the 1941 MECO building, whose rooftop garden serves the daycare centre it houses. Here what is most notable is the relationship of each of the building's façades to the street and of the building as a whole to the *quartier*.

The building's innovative double-skin technology permits circulation and recycling of air in the ten-centimetre-wide void between the double-glazed curtain wall on the exterior and the single-glazed shutter layer on the interior. The building's "greenness" is discreetly expressed and directed towards providing natural light and fresh air to office workers.

Architects	**Gauthier Daoust Lestage Inc. / FABG / Lemay et Associés**
Client	**Caisse de dépôt et placement du Québec**
Completed	**2003**
Address	**1000 Place Jean-Paul Riopelle**
Métro	**Square-Victoria–OACI or Place-d'Armes**
Access	**lobby only – open weekdays during business hours**

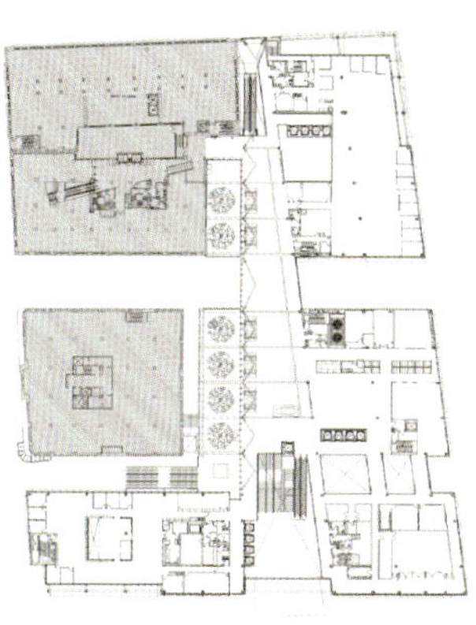
Place Riopelle

UNITY 2

Unity 2 has introduced itself to the Quartier international de Montréal with ease and inventiveness. Built to adjoin the Unity Building (designed by architect David Spence in 1912 and converted to condos in 2001), the L-shaped structure creates an intriguing semi-public interior courtyard. In total, there are five different types of units in Unity 2 – the majority are two-level "flo-thru" units, with windows onto both the courtyard and the street. The complex topological challenge of the building is only hinted at by the very unassuming brick-panel façade.

The wooden-decked courtyard, designed by NIPpaysage, is a revelation as one looks through the gate from the street. A dramatic industrial-strength exit stair dominates the space on the east side of the courtyard, and five ground-level townhouses front onto it.

Unity 3, also designed by Atelier Big City, was added in 2015 on de la Gauchetière, sliding in between the Unity Building and a brick extension to the AIMIA tower. Its zigzag façade of projecting windows is playful but not as clearly articulated as Unity 2.

Unity 3

Architects	**Atelier Big City**
Landscape architect	**NIPpaysage**
Client	**Les Développements D'Arcy McGee Ltée**
Completed	**2005**
Address	**445 Av. Viger Ouest**
Métro	**Square-Victoria–OACI or Place-d'Armes**
Access	**exterior only**

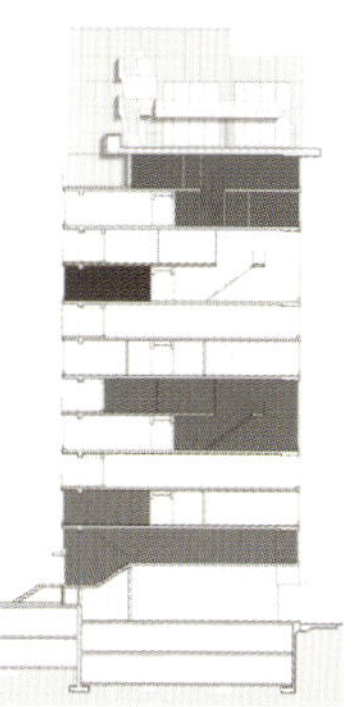

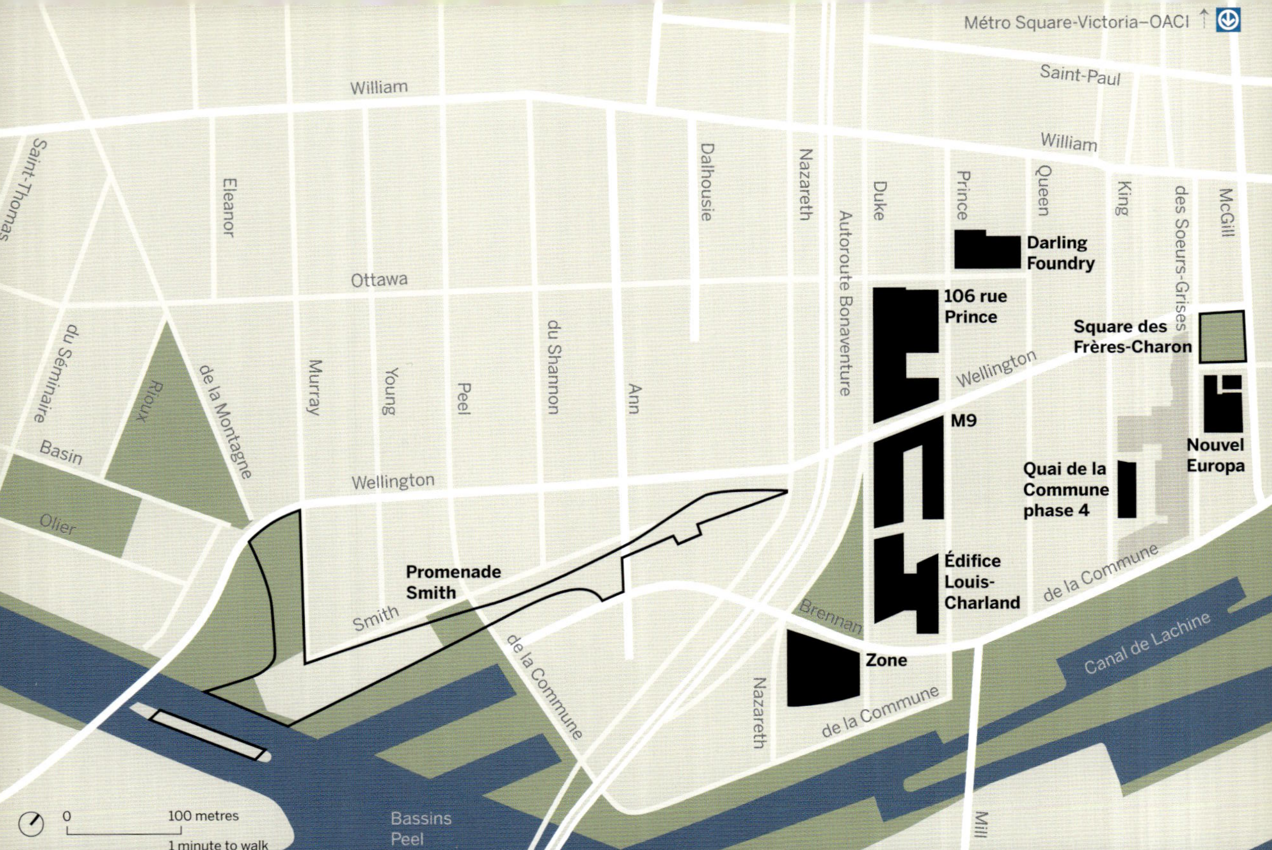

Métro Square-Victoria–OACI
Saint-Paul
William
William
Saint-Thomas
Eleanor
Dalhousie
Nazareth
Autoroute Bonaventure
Duke
Prince
Queen
King
des Soeurs-Grises
McGill
Darling Foundry
106 rue Prince
Square des Frères-Charon
Ottawa
Wellington
M9
Nouvel Europa
Quai de la Commune phase 4
du Séminaire
Rioux
de la Montagne
Murray
Young
Peel
du Shannon
Ann
Basin
Wellington
Olier
Édifice Louis-Charland
de la Commune
Promenade Smith
Smith
Brennan
de la Commune
Zone
Canal de Lachine
Nazareth
de la Commune
Bassins Peel
Mill
0
100 metres
1 minute to walk

FAUBOURG DES RÉCOLLETS / GRIFFINTOWN

Faubourg des Récollets, immediately to the west of the formerly fortified city, sits at the mouth of the Lachine Canal and was the first section industrialized following the canal's construction in 1825. Griffintown, the sector between William and de la Commune and extending to the west to de la Montagne, was home to the many Irish immigrants who built the canal and who, in the 1880s, worked in the foundries when Montreal was truly the metropolis of Canada.

The Bonaventure expressway, built in 1967, sliced through the *quartier*, and with the closure of the Lachine Canal in 1970, the area was largely abandoned by the 1980s. In the Faubourg des Récollets, artists took over the empty factories and warehouses and ultimately were responsible for the regeneration of the *quartier*. *Panique au Faubourg*, a 1997 series of urban installations that included projecting images on the full height of the silos, and the multimedia company Discreet Logic's decision the same year to convert the Weir building into offices marked the turning point for the area. The City of Montreal, having bought many of the disused industrial buildings in the early 1990s, created Cité Multimédia, a private-public information technology development in 1998.

Griffintown is undergoing a massive transformation. Development has been largely privately financed and planning of the *quartier* has only been "applied" after the fact. Multiple condominium developments are marching across the neighbourhood, which retains very few vestiges of its industrial past.

DARLING FOUNDRY

From 1889 to 1971, the Darling Foundry complex produced industrial equipment. Sold to pump manufacturers, it was finally abandoned in 1991 and sat empty for a decade. The choice of architects Atelier in situ to convert the 1200-square-metre space into a contemporary art centre was a logical one, given their 1997 experience with the Zone project at the southernmost edge of the Faubourg des Récollets. The architects' strategy was to let the morphology of the building define its reuse – the three-storey-high shop now serves as the gallery's multi-functional space, lit by the immense windows that served the factory. Offices are on the second floor; a drywalled area beneath serves as a more traditional gallery. A café/art space runs the length of the Prince façade.

Intervention in this project is simultaneously strong and minimalist, dictated both by budget constraints and by a desire to let the building speak for itself. Inset drywall panels define the edges and let the structure show.

In 2006, the eastern section of the building was converted by the architectural consortium of L'OEUF and Desnoyers Mercure to living quarters and studios for Quartier Éphémère's artists-in-residence program.

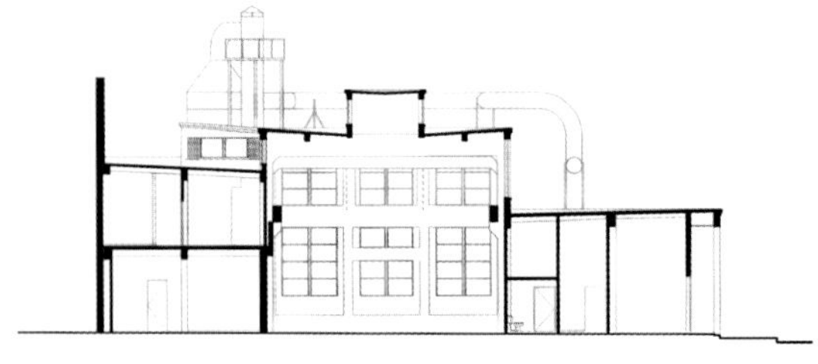

Architects	**Atelier in situ**
Client	**Quartier Éphémère**
Completed	**2002**
Address	**745 Rue Ottawa**
Métro	**Square-Victoria–OACI (+ bus 61 sud)**
Access	**open to public during gallery hours**

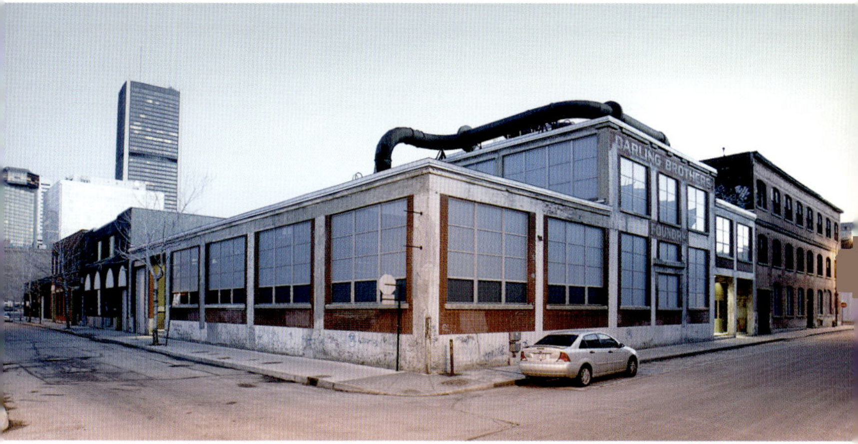
DARLING BROTHERS
FOUNDRY

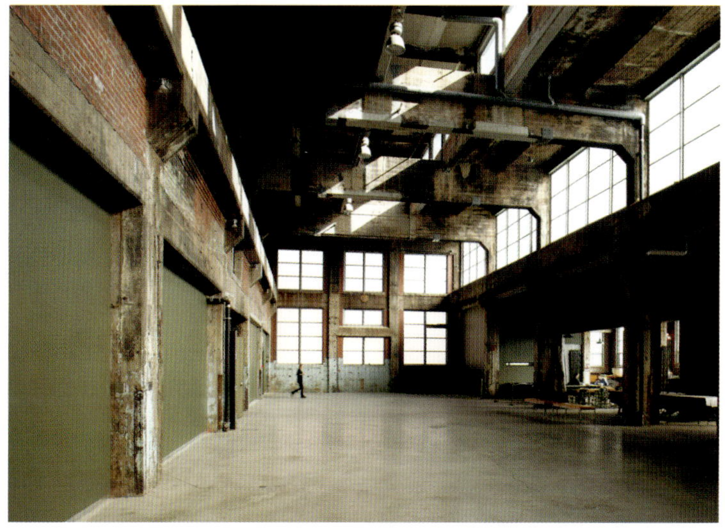

106 RUE PRINCE

Cité Multimédia, the government-financed redevelopment of the southern part of Faubourg des Récollets, includes both new construction and projects that integrate existing industrial structures. In 106 Prince, Phase 4 of Cité Multimédia, two Darling Foundry buildings across the street from the foundry proper anchor the north end of the complex. New construction is very effectively woven into the fabric of early-20th-century brick structures. A garden/courtyard on the Prince side defines an east-west axis through the building's capacious lobby space. Judicious use of materials and careful attention to detail are evident at this ground-floor-level intersection of public and tenant use.

The Bonaventure expressway, built as an elevated highway in 1966, defines the western edge of both 106 Prince and the Edifice Louis-Charland. A six-year-long project to lower the expressway to grade will be complete by 2017 and will undoubtedly change how the two buildings are perceived.

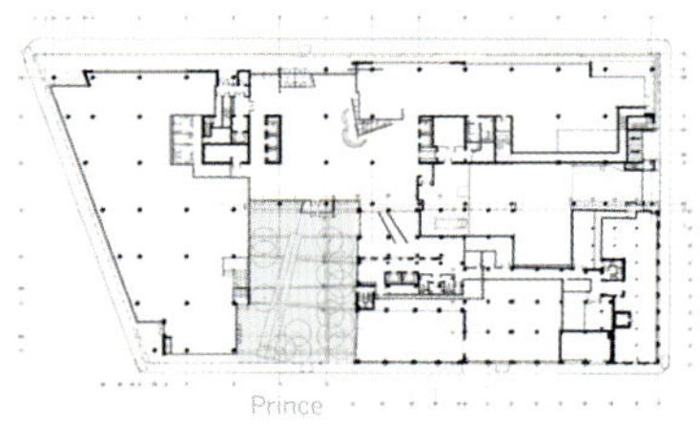

Architects	**Cardinal Hardy / Provencher Roy et Associés**
Client	**SDM / SITQ Immobilier / SOLIM**
Completed	**2000**
Address	**106 Rue Prince**
Métro	**Square-Victoria–OACI (+ bus 61 sud)**
Access	**interior – lobby only**

EDIFICE LOUIS-CHARLAND

Like 106 Rue Prince, this building has to present two faces to the world. It must announce the presence of the revitalized *quartier* to those driving along the Bonaventure expressway, and it must relate to the late-19th-century scale of the original industrial area. The architects' response was to create two distinct, staggered volumes, linked by a glazed atrium space.

The eight-storey-high west façade on Duke provides all the desired drama with its ceramic-fritted glass screen – remarkable when it reflects winter sunlight or lit up at night. The smaller volume on Prince is clad in slate-coloured brick on the lower four stories and zinc on the fifth. The lobby joining the two is oriented north-south and is intended to act as the gateway to the neighbourhood. The entrance from Brennan is suitably welcoming, but the Prince entry is not as successful.

Architects	**Menkès Shooner Dagenais / Dupuis LeTourneux**
Client	**La Société en commandite Brennan-Duke, Cité Multimédia – Lot 2**
Completed	**2001**
Address	**801 Rue Brennan**
Métro	**Square-Victoria–OACI (+ bus 61 sud)**
Access	**interior – lobby only**

M9 CONDOMINIUMS

A shot of colour in the Faubourg des Récollets, this four-phase condominium project wraps around the block of Wellington between Duke and Prince. Acid-green metal frames identify individual units on the Prince façade, then define the base of the tower on Wellington. Large square openings, evoking the *porte-cochères* of a much earlier Montreal housing type, have been cut through the slender building to an interior courtyard.

Architects	**NOMADE, Sid Lee architecture (Phase 3 with Aedifica)**
Client	**DevMcGill**
Completed	**2007–15**
Address	**Rues Prince / Wellington / Duke**
Métro	**Square-Victoria–OACI (+ bus 61 sud)**
Access	**exterior only**

ZONE

According to the architects, this project was all about letting the building reveal itself. They deftly recycled a heavy industrial building to serve as the headquarters of a multimedia company. The relentlessly functional exterior was left intact, except for the huge Cor-Ten panels that replace the original doors, with an entry inserted between the two. New steel windows were fitted into the original openings.

The massive interior volumes that once accommodated the manufacture of ship sections – two large halls that were built around an earlier brick factory structure – now house workstations. Material interventions include steel railings, polished concrete floors and maple doors to define public versus private spaces.

It is not an exaggeration to say that this project generated the revitalization of the Faubourg des Récollets. The energy invested by owner and architects (who worked onsite throughout the project) attracted both public and private development to the former industrial area.

Architects	**Atelier in situ**
Client	**Discreet Logic**
Completed	**1997**
Address	**10 Rue Duke**
Métro	**Square-Victoria–OACI (+bus 61 sud)**
Access	**interior – lobby only**

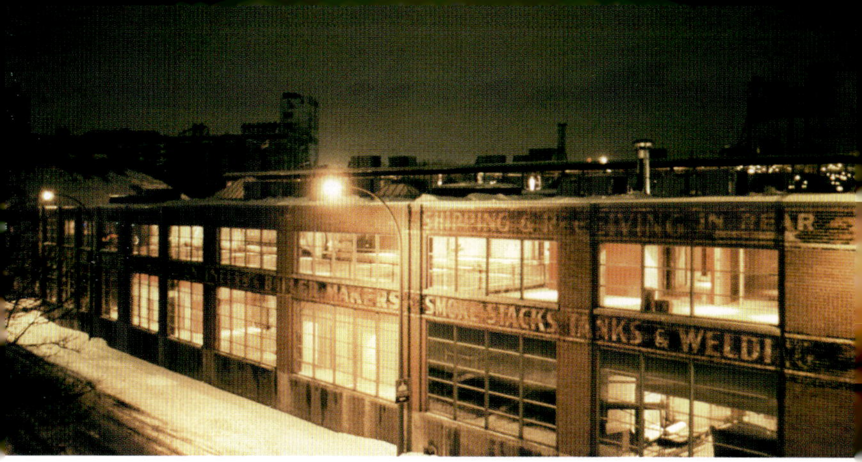
MAKERS
SMOKESTACKS
TANKS &

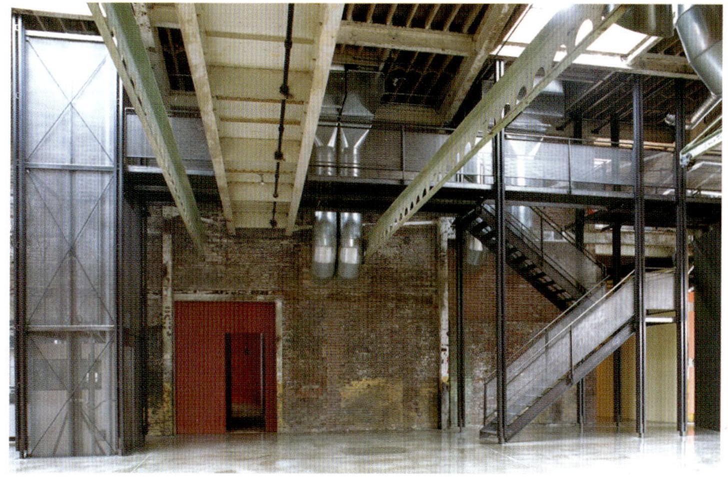

QUAI DE LA COMMUNE PHASE 4

This complex features new construction and reuse of existing buildings, including two early-20th-century warehouses. In all, 325 units of lofts and apartments were built in five phases over six years, in the block between King and des Soeurs-Grises. Of special interest – because of the way it sets itself apart from the typical Montreal housing type – is a series of ten brick-and-concrete-block rowhouse/studios fronting on King.

Doorways are recessed and fenestration is appropriately industrial. Each building is three storeys tall, with exceptionally high ceilings and large windows overlooking a common interior courtyard.

Architects	**Cardinal Hardy**
Client	**Le Groupe Prével**
Completed	**2003**
Address	**41-59 Rue King**
Métro	**Square-Victoria–OACI (+ bus 61 sud)**
Access	**exterior only**

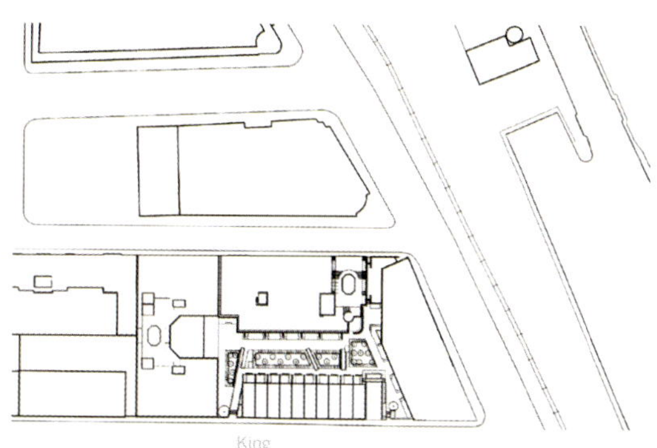
King

SQUARE DES FRÈRES-CHARON

Like a railway turntable, this square is a connector between the formerly walled city of Old Montreal, McGill St. that runs down its western edge and the Faubourg des Récollets. Deceptively simple, the square speaks to the 17th-century origins of the site, a meadow with a windmill to grind grain owned by the Charon brothers, and to successive layers of history. The granite paving creates a circular shape and ties it to the granite pavers of Old Montreal, and the cylindrical folly with belvedere conceals the access to a major water collector twenty metres below grade. Planting is exceptionally conscious of the four seasons.

Product of a multidisciplinary team process organized by the Arrondissement Ville-Marie that included online public consultations, this project could have been incoherent; it's to everyone's credit that it is a clear and legible public space.

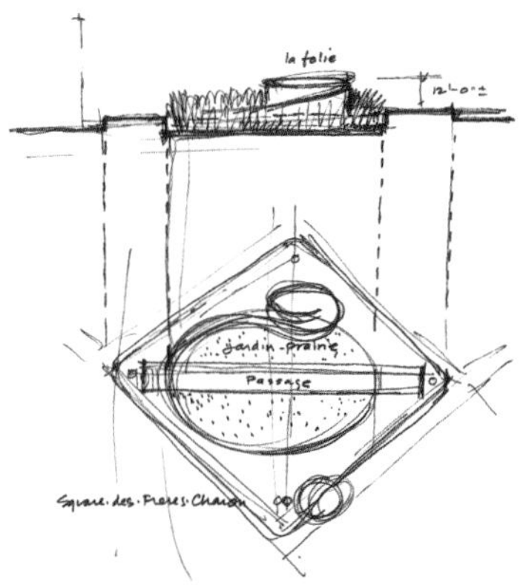

Architects **Affleck + de la Riva**
Landscape architect **Robert Desjardins**
Artist **Raphaëlle de Groot**
Client **Arrondissement Ville-Marie**
Completed **2009**
Address **corner Rue McGill and Wellington**
Métro **Square-Victoria–OACI (+ bus 61 sud)**
Access **public**

NOUVEL EUROPA

The site of the Nouvel Europa, near the foot of McGill St., was a shipyard in the 1800s, then the railhead for the 1923 Union Station – a tiny brick structure that has been integrated into the project. The shape of the new construction is deceptively simple: a large rectangular box with a base and cornice like those of the 19th-century financial and transportation buildings to the north.

The construction is actually two buildings around a central courtyard, the base of which forms the roof slab over the commercial space. Each through-unit apartment has both a street face and a private courtyard side. Two glazed pedestrian walkways traverse the space; the one at the north end is partially obscured by a semi-transparent screen fritted with black ceramic traces of the rail lines as they were in 1918. The façade is best viewed from farther up McGill St.

The Square des Frères-Charon, north of the site, has been completely revamped. The infrastructure, sidewalks and civic spaces of McGill St. were redesigned by the consortium responsible for the Quartier international de Montréal, providing a long-needed new face for one of Old Montreal's most significant streets.

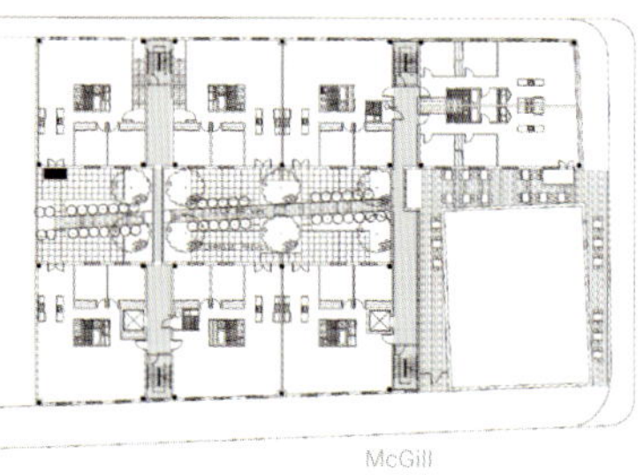

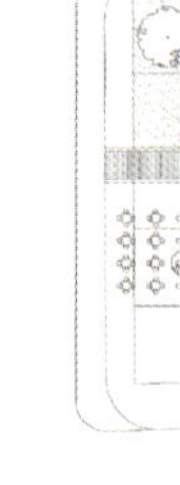

Architects	**Boutros + Pratte**
Client	**Jean-Pierre Houle**
Completed	**2004**
Address	**600 Rue D'Youville**
Metro	**Square-Victoria–OACI (+ bus 61 sud)**
Access	**exterior only**

PROMENADE SMITH

Planning Griffintown's public spaces has required fitting them into and around the private developments. Here the strategy for this new public space to be completed in 2017 is to follow Smith, a road that slides along the railway track. A two-stage architectural competition in 2011 elicited *Granny Smith*, described by the winners, landscape architects NIPpaysage, as "a hybrid between a garden, a street, a park and a public space." This project has been – exceptionally – included in the book because, though not yet complete, it will have a significant impact on the neighbourhood.

As a result of a second competition in spring 2015, the architectural consortium of Beaupré Michaud / SHED will convert the Wellington signal box located at the western limit of the public space into a café and incubator creative space, to be completed by 2017.

Landscape Architect	**NIPpaysage**
Client	**Ville de Montréal**
Completed	**2017**
Address	**follows Rue Smith from Rue Nazareth to de la Montagne**
Métro	**Bonaventure (+ bus 107 sud)**
Access	**public**

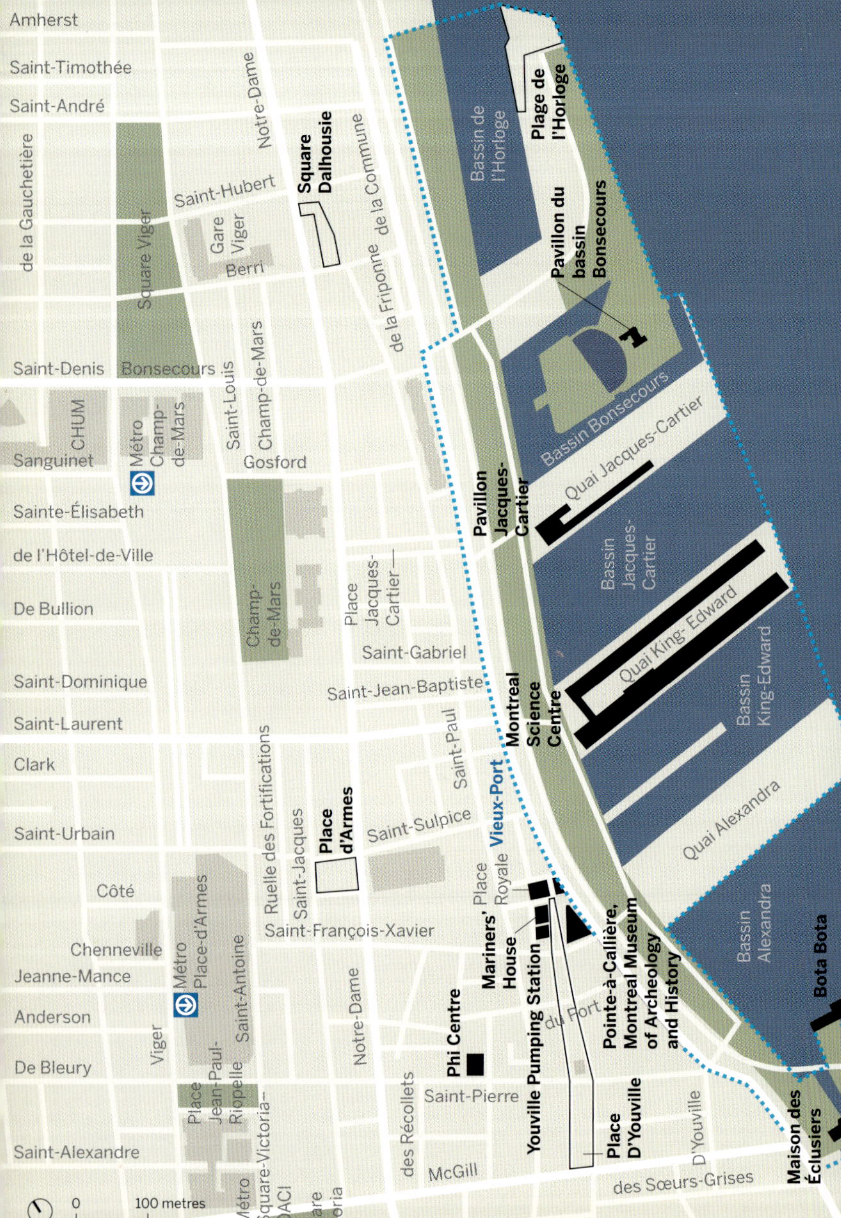

Amherst
Saint-Timothée
Saint-André
de la Gauchetière
Notre-Dame
Square Dalhousie
de la Commune
Saint-Hubert
Square Viger
Gare Viger
Berri
de la Friponne
Bassin de l'Horloge
Plage de l'Horloge
Pavillon du bassin Bonsecours
Saint-Denis
Bonsecours
Saint-Louis
Champ-de-Mars
CHUM
Métro Champ-de-Mars
Bassin Bonsecours
Quai Jacques-Cartier
Sanguinet
Gosford
Pavillon Jacques-Cartier
Sainte-Élisabeth
de l'Hôtel-de-Ville
Place Jacques-Cartier
Champ-de-Mars
Bassin Jacques-Cartier
De Bullion
Saint-Gabriel
Quai King-Edward
Saint-Dominique
Saint-Jean-Baptiste
Montreal Science Centre
Bassin King-Edward
Saint-Laurent
Saint-Paul
Clark
Ruelle des Fortifications
Vieux-Port
Saint-Jacques
Place d'Armes
Saint-Sulpice
Saint-Urbain
Quai Alexandra
Place Royale
Côté
Métro Place-d'Armes
Saint-François-Xavier
Mariners' House
Chenneville
Jeanne-Mance
Saint-Antoine
Notre-Dame
Pointe-à-Callière, Montreal Museum of Archeology and History
Bassin Alexandra
Bota Bota
Anderson
Viger
Phi Centre
Youville Pumping Station
du Fort
De Bleury
Place Jean-Paul-Riopelle
des Récollets
Saint-Pierre
Place D'Youville
D'Youville
Maison des Éclusiers
Saint-Alexandre
McGill
des Sœurs-Grises
0
100 metres
1 minute to walk
Métro Square-Victoria–OACI
Square Victoria

OLD MONTREAL / OLD PORT / FAUBOURG QUÉBEC

There are a few traces of the 18th-century fortified city built by the French, but most of the remarkable densely built ensemble of greystone buildings that is present-day Old Montreal dates from the 19th century, the era when Montreal was the metropolis of Canada.

Old Montreal was at its lowest ebb in the 1960s. The 1959 opening of the Seaway had diminished the city's role as Canada's principal port and the *quartier* was reduced to rooming houses and warehouses. The 1964 declaration of the sector as an *arrondissement historique* staved off demolition, but revitalization was limited to individual restoration projects, mostly to mark Canada's centennial in 1967, the year of the World's Fair, Expo 67.

Habitat 67 was built as part of Expo 67 and was the first contemporary intervention in the port. Relocation of the working port to the east in the 1970s meant that much of the infrastructure was abandoned or demolished; the Old Port was created as a separate entity in 1981 by the federal government to oversee redevelopment of the waterfront. The first phase of the revitalization project, completed in 1992, created new public urban spaces for cultural and recreational purposes.

East of Berri, Faubourg Québec was a suburb immediately outside the walls in the 18th century and home to the bourgeoisie in the first half of the 19th. The construction of two train stations in the 1880s and 1890s led to complete industrialization of the area, now redeveloped as residential around Dalhousie Station while Viger Station has been transformed into office space.

PLACE D'YOUVILLE

To create a new landscape for one of the most historically intense public places in Montreal, Claude Cormier and Cardinal Hardy simply laid what they describe as a "quilt of sidewalks" on top of Place D'Youville. Here, at the site of the founding of Montreal, the archaeological strata are many and run deep at the place where the Petite Rivière Saint-Pierre ran into the St. Lawrence River. In 1832, the little river was vaulted over and markets were built on top.

Practically – to avoid disturbing artefacts – and philosophically – to not just slavishly recreate history, the design is more about movement across and along the long ribbon that extends from the Centre d'histoire (a 1902 fire station) to de la Commune. A granite-paved walk, a "collector of pedestrians," runs down the centre of the Place, evoking the stone conduit of the water collector below. Wooden, limestone and concrete sidewalks cut diagonally across this spine, evoking the domestic, commercial and institutional buildings that line the Place.

Architects	**Cardinal Hardy**
Landscape architect	**Claude Cormier**
Client	**Ville de Montréal, Ministère de la Culture et des Communications du Québec**
Completed	**1999**
Address	**Place D'Youville between Place Royale and McGill**
Métro	**Place-d'Armes**
Access	**public**

POINTE-À-CALLIÈRE

Montreal Museum of Archaeology and History

The site of the Pointe-à-Callière museum is the triangle of land where de Maisonneuve founded Montreal in 1642 – historical significance so important as to be daunting. The triangular Éperon was built directly on top of more than four centuries of archaeological remains, preserved and exposed below ground. The ensemble of the Éperon building, the crypt under Place Royale and the 1836 Ancienne-Douane constitutes the original core of the Museum of Archaeology and History, built in 1992 to celebrate Montreal's 350th anniversary.

Clad in the limestone, out of which Montreal was built, and pierced with vertical slots, the Éperon building succeeds at every level: it respects utterly the streetscape of Old Montreal, pays homage to the port and alludes to the 1862 Royal Insurance Building that formerly occupied the site. Resolutely contemporary, the structure occupies its corner with absolute assurance, its sliced-cylinder tower a signal to the whole Old Port.

The interior contains a theatre dedicated to an audiovisual presentation of Montreal's history, exhibition spaces, offices and a restaurant on the top floor whose belvedere offers a great view of the Old Port. Access to the crypt and former customs house is via a tunnel under Place D'Youville. To provide headroom for the crypt, Place Royale had to be raised above grade, resulting in a curious podium with glazed horizontal slits.

An ambitious expansion plan for the museum will create a complex using the William collector sewer that runs underneath Place D'Youville as an underground connector to a series of new sites to be added starting with Fort Ville-Marie, site of the first European settlement.

Architects **Dan S. Hanganu / Provencher Roy (Éperon and crypt)**
LeMoyne Lapointe Magne (Ancienne-Douane)
Client **Ville de Montréal**
Completed **1992**
Address **350 Place Royale**
Métro **Square-Victoria–OACI or Place-d'Armes**
Access **see website**

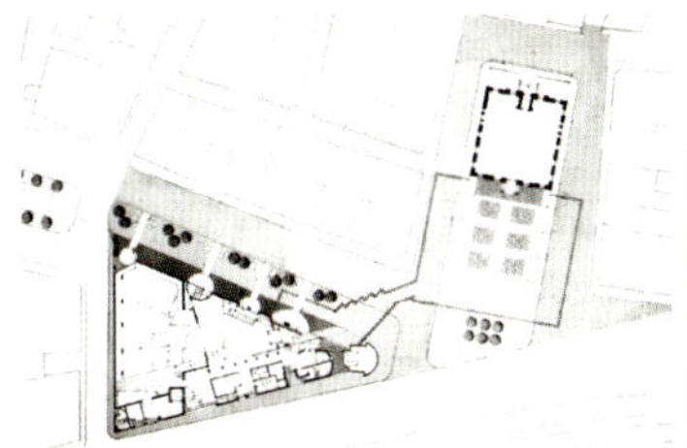

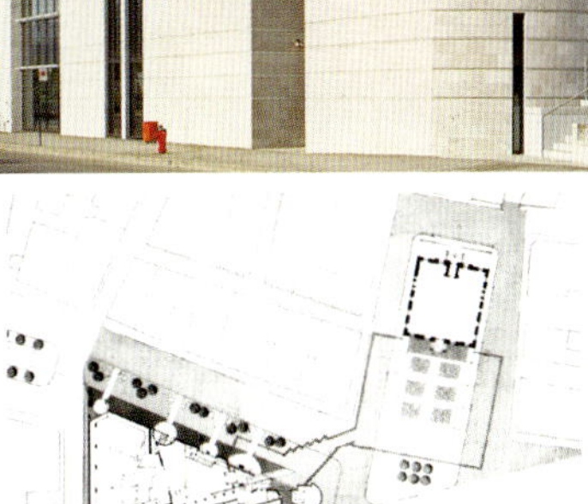

POINTE-À-CALLIÈRE

Youville Pumping Station

The modest 1913 structure that housed Montreal's first electrically run wastewater pumping station closed in 1990. Acquired by the Société du Musée d'archéologie, the building was converted and added onto in 1999 to create an interpretation centre for the adjacent Pointe-à-Callière museum. Intervention in the pumping station proper was light handed, limited to cleaning the brick and painting the three large pumps housed there red.

Construction on a vacant lot to the west of the pumping station provided room for archives, elevator, services and office space on the second floor. Matte zinc-titanium panels on the façade frame the yellow-orange Scottish brick of the pumping station – a thoughtful addition to the streetscape in a very visible part of Old Montreal.

Architects	**Dupuis LeTourneux / Beauchamp Bourbeau**
Client	**Pointe-à-Callière, Montréal Museum of Archaeology and History**
Completed	**1999**
Address	**173 Place D'Youville**
Métro	**Square-Victoria–OACI or Place-d'Armes**
Access	**see website**

Mariners' House

The original programme for the Musée d'archéologie focused on the archaeological remains – little space for temporary exhibitions was included. With the addition to the museum complex of the 1953 Mariners' House, three thousand square metres of space solve the problem and add educational spaces. Archaeological excavations under the building are linked to the main crypt under Place Royale.

The intriguing aspect of this renovation project is the modification of a modest post-war structure so that it both has a contemporary presence and speaks to the 1992 Epéron building directly opposite. A two-storey-high glazed curtain wall hits the right note of respecting the building's context and its role in the museum complex.

Architects	**Dan S. Hanganu / Provencher Roy**
Client	**Pointe-à-Callière Musée d'archéologie et d'histoire de Montréal / Quartier international de Montréal**
Completed	**2012**
Address	**165 Place D'Youville**
Métro	**Square-Victoria–OACI or Place-d'Armes**
Access	**see website**

PHI CENTRE

Inserting a complex programme into two adjoining 19th-century greystone buildings to serve as stages for installation and performance spaces was a demanding mandate. Doing it minimally, using contemporary materials, Atelier in situ designed two theatres that are flexible, versatile and acoustically separate. In addition, studio spaces, a production suite and a multi-function space are stacked and electronically linked; from the polished concrete and glass lobby, a central skylit core pierces through to the roof with its extraordinary terrace.

The envelope was restored by Shapiro Wolfe, who also designed a green roof/rainwater collection system, among other sustainable features.

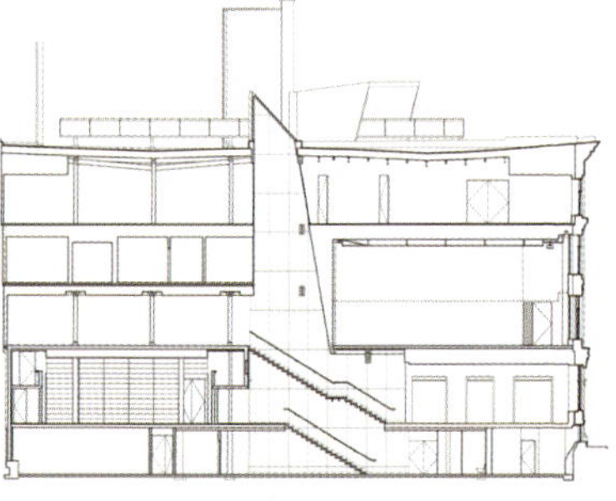

Architects	**Atelier in situ / Shapiro Wolfe**
Client	**Centre PHI / Phoebe Greenberg**
Completed	**2012**
Address	**407 Rue Saint-Pierre**
Métro	**Square-Victoria–OACI or Place D'Armes**
Access	**see website**

PLACE D'ARMES

The rebuilt Place d'Armes is European in character, based on a model of sharing urban space that is atypical for Montreal. While the square functions as the principal meeting point for visitors to Old Montreal, it is also surrounded by a constant flow of traffic, so the choice of one continuous level for street, sidewalk and square in front of Notre-Dame Basilica was met with some apprehension. Bollards do help to separate pedestrians from cars, but the reality is that the sharing is so obvious as to make each aware of the other.

The core idea for the redesign of one of the oldest public spaces in Montreal – first established in the 17th century, site of the 1685 Sulpician Seminary, the 1829 Notre-Dame Basilica, the 1847 Bank of Montreal and much more – was the "memory of the stone." The granite pavers, new and recovered, delineate the streets and the footprint of the first Notre-Dame church.

The monument to de Maisonneuve, the focal point of the Victorian square when it was erected in 1895, was restored as part of the 2011 rebuilding. The street furniture by designer Michel Morelli is interesting, both generous in size and thoughtful in placement. The large platform-like bench at the northeast corner also serves to close off the access to underground washrooms, a public facility that was added in the 1930s.

As a public space so imbued with historical meaning, it is refreshing to see it crisply and confidently redesigned.

Architects	**Groupe IBI-CHBA / Ville de Montréal, Direction des grands parcs**
Client	**Ville de Montréal**
Completed	**2011**
Address	**Rue Notre-Dame**
Métro	**Place-d'Armes**
Access	**public**

OLD PORT

In the 1970s, port operations moved to the east, away from Montreal's harbour, which had been in use since the 17th century. The many proposals that were put forward on how to redevelop the 53 hectares of the old port succeeded only in creating controversy. Public consultations held in 1985–86 – perhaps the most successful in the city's history – generated the themes upon which the 1990 master plan was based: a port, a historic place and public use.

Letting the history of the place speak for itself meant retaining industrial structures such as Silo #5 and, more pragmatically, keeping the existing rail link to the container port. Traces such as the vestiges of Silo #2's foundations are matter-of-factly integrated. Contemporary interventions, like the Pavillon Jacques-Cartier and the ensemble of street furniture, railings, bollards and lamp standards, are sober and beautifully scaled.

The first phase of the Old Port revitalization was completed in time for the city's 350th anniversary in 1992. It included excavation and restoration of both the Bonsecours Basin and the western sector at the mouth of the Lachine Canal, as well as construction along the length of de la Commune. The other quays have been refurbished since, including the King Edward pier for the Montreal Science Centre.

The linear park acts simultaneously as access to and relief from Old Montreal for tourists, and as a place to walk and cycle for Montrealers – their window on the river.

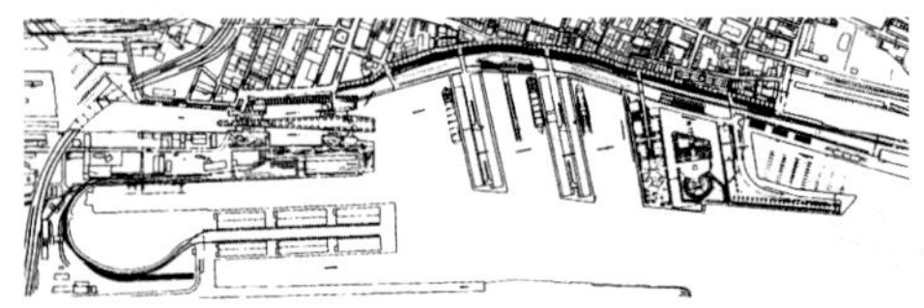

Architects	**Cardinal Hardy et Associés / Peter Rose / Jodoin Lamarre Pratte et Associés (master plan)**
Client	**Société du Vieux-Port de Montréal**
Completed	**1993**
Address	**mouth of Lachine Canal to Faubourg Québec**
Métro	**Square-Victoria–OACI or Place-d'Armes or Champ-de-Mars**
Access	**public**

Bota Bota

Floating at the end of the Old Port Locks park, a 1951 ferry has found a third life as a Scandinavian spa. Meticulously renovated, the spa both respects its naval heritage and projects the material calm necessary for a spa. Prefabricated metal panels with embedded portholes, metal stairways and exposed structure are juxtaposed with wood decking and cladding. The pleasure of the spa lies as much in the perception of the ship against the extraordinary backdrop of Silo #5 as the solid execution of the project.

Architects	**Sid Lee Architecture**
Client	**Bota Bota, spa-sur-l'eau**
Completed	**2010**
Address	**358 Rue de la Commune Ouest, Quais du Vieux-Port de Montréal**
Métro	**Square-Victoria–OACI or Place-d'Armes**
Access	**exterior only**

Maison des Éclusiers

An integral part of the 1992 Old Port project, the Maison des Éclusiers offers a spectacular view of the mouth of the Lachine Canal and its locks. The industrial language of the pavilion is clearly drawn from the infrastructure of the port – part of the overall intent to let the contemporary construction speak to the port's early-20th-century history. The pavilion houses a café-terrasse in the summer.

Architects **Cardinal Hardy et Associés**
Client **Société du Vieux-Port de Montréal**
Completed **1993**
Address **Rue McGill at de la Commune**
Métro **Square-Victoria–OACI or Place-d'Armes**
Access **seasonal – open end of May to end of September**

Montreal Science Centre

Two immense sheds – with a total area of 500,000 square metres – on the King Edward pier were transformed into a science interpretation centre and parking facility. The volumes were kept simple, and the new exterior double skin is rhythmic and industrial in scale. The service road between the two, an extension of St. Laurent, is lined with recycled containers that open up as shops in the summer.

Architects	**Gauthier Daoust Lestage Inc. / FABG**
Client	**Société du Vieux-Port de Montréal**
Completed	**2000**
Address	**Quai King Edward, Old Port of Montréal**
Metro	**Place-d'Armes**
Access	**see website**

Pavillon Jacques-Cartier

Constructed on the foundations of the great long shed that once stood on this pier, the pavilion evokes the maritime language of the port. An enfilade of steel masts runs the length of the quay, its tension cables supporting a raised walkway. The enclosed large open space for seasonal events is almost entirely glazed, its structure exposed. To the visitor walking down Place Jacques-Cartier from Notre-Dame, the pavilion is the clearest possible signal of the contemporary nature of the Old Port.

Architects **Cardinal Hardy / Cayouette-Chartrand**
Client **Société du Vieux-Port de Montréal**
Completed **1992**
Address **Quai Jacques-Cartier**
Métro **Champ-de-Mars**
Access **seasonal – open end of May to end of September**

Pavillon du bassin Bonsecours

The Bonsecours Basin was excavated in 1992 and a skating rink was built. The skating pavilion is deceptively simple and, with its playful allusion to the 19th-century domes of the old city, a contrast to the industrial language of other Old Port projects. Deliberately over-scaled, its domed roof holds its own in the landscape and signals that the Bonsecours basin is more park than port.

Architect	**Luc Laporte**
Client	**Société du Vieux-Port de Montréal**
Completed	**1992**
Address	**Rue de la Commune Est (Parc du bassin Bonsecours)**
Métro	**Champ-de-Mars**
Access	**public**

Plage de l'Horloge

Located at the easternmost section of the Old Port, the strength of the urban beach's design is immediately evident. Projecting into the waters at the foot of the 1921 clock tower, the beach wraps around the Quai de l'Horloge, the pier that protects the marina. Playful blue parasols, deck chairs, mist showers and all – the installation is soundly detailed and fun. Montrealers would be happier if the beach were accessible year round and with no admission fee.

Landscape architect	**Claude Cormier + associés**
Client	**Société du Vieux-Port de Montréal**
Completed	**2012**
Address	**333 Rue de la Commune Ouest**
Métro	**Champ-de-Mars**
Access	**seasonal (admission fee)**

SQUARE DALHOUSIE

Faubourg Québec was a "suburb" outside the original walled city of Montreal, built at the gate to the road to Quebec City. The whole area – including the original Dalhousie Square – was destroyed by fire in 1852. In the late 19th century, the nascent railways built stations and railyards – the first train to leave for the west departed from Dalhousie Station in 1886.

Square Dalhousie sits on these invisible layers of history and acts as entryway to the 21st-century Faubourg Québec, a 70-hectare redevelopment project by the Société de développement de Montréal. Defined to the north by the former Dalhousie Station and to the south by new residential construction, the square is a narrative: it traces the location of the original fortification walls and incorporates vestiges of the railway era. A sculpture by Jocelyne Alloucherie commemorates the Quebec gate.

Dalhousie Station was imaginatively recycled to house a circus school in 1986 by architect Vianney Bélanger and now houses a circus company.

The Notre Dame viaduct – accessible via a stairway to the east of the station – was rebuilt by architects Dupuis LeTourneux with Saia Barbarese in 1997. Described as a "bridge building," it is intended as both roadway and outlook, with a view of the whole *faubourg* and the river beyond.

Immediately to the north is Viger Station, the 1898 château-style railway station-hotel now converted to loft-style offices.

Architects	**Ville de Montréal (principal designer Robert Desjardins)**
Client	**Ville de Montréal**
Completed	**2004**
Address	**Rue Berri below Rue Notre-Dame**
Métro	**Champ-de-Mars**
Access	**public**

Quai de l'Horloge
Pont Jacques-Ca
Stewart Museum
Île Sainte-Hélène
Chemin du Tour-de-l'Isle
Métro Jean-Drapeau
Biosphere
Pont de la Concorde
Parc Jean-Drapeau
Lac des Cygnes
Chemin MacDonald
Fleuve Saint-Laurent
Île Notre-Dame
Bassin olympique
Voie maritime du Saint-Laurent
Parc de la Voie Maritime
Saint-Lambert
0
200 metres
2 minutes to walk

PARC JEAN-DRAPEAU

Île Ste. Hélène has been used as a park by Montrealers since 1874, accessible first by ferry then via the Jacques Cartier bridge built in 1930. Frederick Todd, the landscape architect responsible for the area around Beaver Lake on Mount Royal, redesigned the island in the 1930s, when as part of the city's make-work projects at the height of the Depression, a swimmers' pavilion and a tower were built next to the 1820 citadel constructed by the British.

Île Ste. Hélène and the man-made Île Notre-Dame were the site of Expo 67, the World's Fair that marked Canada's centennial. Very little built form remains of that glorious summer, with the exception of the Biosphere, and that which does remain is no longer recognizable.

The islands (renamed Parc Jean-Drapeau to honour the mayor who brought Expo 67 to Montreal) now include many recreational activities. Île Ste. Hélène has a swimming pool complex and La Ronde, an amusement park that first opened as part of Expo 67; Île Notre-Dame is home to the Grand Prix racetrack and the Olympic rowing basin.

A massive amphitheatre on the western sector of Île Ste. Hélène as well as an extension to the metro station concourse leading to Calder's monumental *L'homme* sculpture and a riverside promenade are planned for completion by 2019.

BIOSPHERE

Intervention or conservation? A spectacular fire in 1976 destroyed the acrylic skin of Buckminster Fuller's geodesic dome, built as the American pavilion for Expo 67, and it sat empty and rusting until 1992. Environment Canada undertook to reopen the structure as an interpretation centre focused on the idea of water – and specifically on the St. Lawrence River ecosystem. The architectural competition required that the existing platform structure be maintained.

Éric Gauthier's design is utterly respectful – both of the mandate and of Fuller – and at the same time assertive in its own right. The paradox of having to provide inwardly focused exhibition space while maximizing natural light and the dome's presence is neatly resolved. What Gauthier gives us is the *experience* of moving through the structure. From a low pavilion at grade, one moves up around a central courtyard to the belvedere, all while being engulfed by the iconic skeleton of Fuller's dome.

In 2010, two roof surfaces within the dome were greened by architects Smith Vigeant – both levels are visible from the belvedere. The emphasis on sustainability is consistent with the Biosphere's broadened mandate, defined as environmental issues.

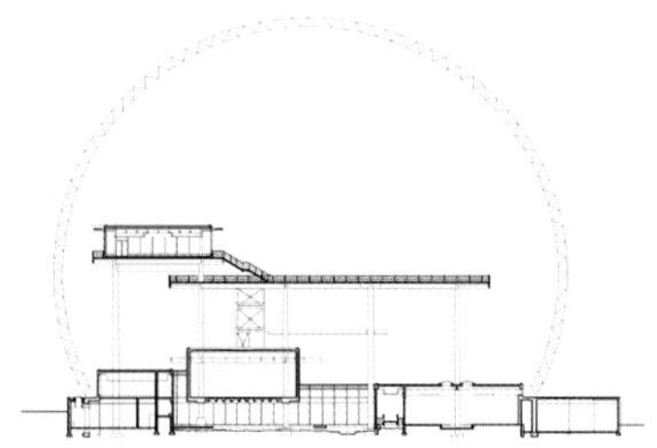

Architects	**Blouin Faucher Aubertin Brodeur Gauthier / Desnoyers Mercure et Associés**
Client	**Environment Canada and Ville de Montréal**
Completed	**1994**
Address	**160 Chemin du Tour-de-l'Isle**
Métro	**Jean-Drapeau**
Access	**see website**

STEWART MUSEUM

The contrast of the glazed cylinder to the limestone of the 19th-century arsenal built by the British is very explicit. The pragmatic need to provide access to the Stewart Museum, housed in the former military structure, becomes a gesture, as a stairway wraps around a mirrored elevator core inside the contemporary structure. At the top level, a belvedere provides a place to view and understand the strategic setting of the fort.

The project also included significant renovations to the museum interior, carefully done so as to both respect the integrity of the building and revamp the exhibition space. The Stewart and McCord Museums signed a merger agreement in 2013, linking two of the most significant collections of historical objects in Montreal.

Architects	**FABG**
Client	**Stewart Museum**
Completed	**2011**
Address	**20 Chemin du Tour-de-l'Isle**
Métro	**Jean-Drapeau**
Access	**see website**

Pavillon du Jardin des Premières-Nations
Insectarium
Jardin botanique
Sherbrooke
d'Orléans
Charlemagne
Jeanne-d'Arc
Rio Tinto Alcan Planetarium
Parc Maisonneuve
Pierre-de-Coubertin
Métro Pie-IX
Métro Viau
Hochelaga
Pie-IX
Desjardins
de la Salle
Letourneux
Bennet
Aird
Sicard
Leclaire
Théodore
Saint-Clément
Viau
de Rouen
Maison de la culture Maisonneuve
Ontario
La Fontaine
Morgan
William-David
0
200 metres
2 minutes to walk

HOCHELAGA-MAISONNEUVE / JARDIN BOTANIQUE

Once a tiny village, Hochelaga was industrialized very rapidly in the last quarter of the 19th century and annexed by the City of Montreal in 1883. The 1905 construction by Canadian Pacific Railway of the immense Angus Shops in neighbouring Rosemont made the northern section of Hochelaga an enclave of workers' housing.

A group of wealthy industrialist-landowners resisted the annexation of the eastern section of Hochelaga and created the town of Maisonneuve. By 1915, huge factories like American Can and Dominion Textile had made the area "Canada's Pittsburgh." A remarkable, ambitious (and ultimately ruinously expensive) 1910 plan was intended to make Maisonneuve a model city, strongly influenced by the American "City Beautiful" movement. Evidence of this plan can still be seen in the width of Morgan Blvd. and the significant public buildings that include a city hall, public baths and a market. The First World War brought financial collapse to Maisonneuve, and the town was annexed to Montreal in 1918.

The Botanical Gardens (Jardin Botanique) were established in Parc Maisonneuve in the 1930s – the work of landscape architect Henry Teuscher and horticulturalist Frère Marie-Victorin. The park is also the site of the 1976 Olympics installations, including the infamous stadium, the "Big O," and the velodrome that was converted into the Biodome in 1992. How to give the Olympic site a new life has preoccupied the city for decades. Following extensive consultations in 2012, a strategy to give the whole park coherence was developed – Space for Life / Espace pour la vie regroups the Biodome, the Insectarium, the Botanical Gardens and the Planetarium.

Like other industrial neighbourhoods, Hochelaga and Maisonneuve have both experienced the conversion of factories to condominiums, most notably around Place Valois created on the site of a former railway line.

MAISON DE LA CULTURE MAISONNEUVE

The 1986 decision of Johnson & Johnson to stay and enlarge its existing building on nearby Pie-IX was remarkable for the gesture of confidence it made to the neighbourhood. This intervention in former Fire Station no. 45 demonstrates how much the *quartier* changed in the ensuing twenty years. The shift is further illustrated by the very lively debate that occurred about the Maison de la culture taking over the fire station space from another artistic organization.

While conversion of fire stations has become commonplace in Montreal, this is a particularly elegant example. The new construction to the south of the original 1895 building proclaims itself as confidently different. The glazed structure on a grey brick base houses a dance space, while the original garage accommodates a multi-functional performance and exhibition space.

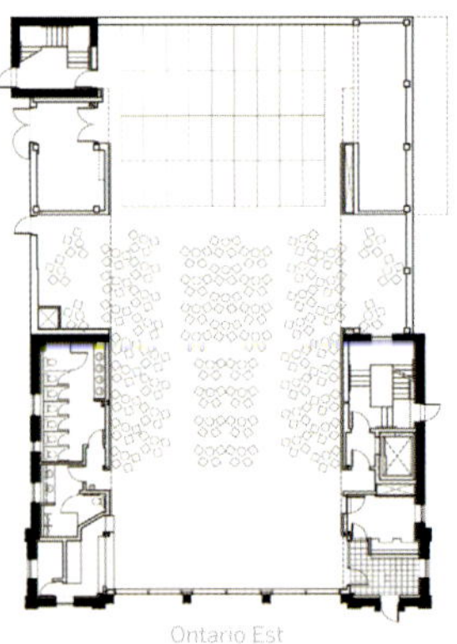

Architects	**FABG**
Client	**Arrondissement Mercier–Hochelaga-Maisonneuve**
Completed	**2005**
Address	**4200 Rue Ontario Est**
Métro	**Pie-IX (+ bus 139 sud)**
Access	**see website**

ESPACE POUR LA VIE – RIO TINTO ALCAN PLANETARIUM

The ongoing challenge to reconfigure the 1976 Olympic site has provoked some encouraging results since 2009. Organizationally, the Biodome, the Insectarium and the Botanical Gardens joined forces as *Espace pour la vie*, a consortium of museums within the larger Parc Maisonneuve / Parc olympique. In 2013, a brand-new planetarium was inserted into the Olympic site, identified as the fourth *Espace pour la vie*.

The chance to design a planetarium is rare indeed. When Montreal decided to hold an international competition to replace the 1966 Dow Planetarium, there were no fewer than sixty-two entries. The site is not an easy one – it is between the Olympic stadium and some municipal sports facilities, just to the north of the Biodome. Walking on the green lichen-clad roof of the planetarium, one is very aware of the looming presence of the two structures.

The most successful part of the planetarium is undoubtedly the two aluminum shingle-clad conical *lunettes* that project skywards, signalling the presence of the two theatres. The interior, which connects to the Biodome at the lower level, is disappointing, despite the maple-slatted volumes of the theatres.

In a bid to update some of the *Espace pour la vie*, three architectural competitions were held in 2014; the Biodome will be renovated starting in 2016 and the Insectarium in 2017, with a new pavilion in the Botanical Gardens to follow at a later date.

Architects	**Cardin Ramirez Julien / Aedifica**
Client	**Ville de Montréal**
Completed	**2013**
Address	**4801 Av. Pierre-de-Coubertin**
Métro	**Viau**
Access	**see website**

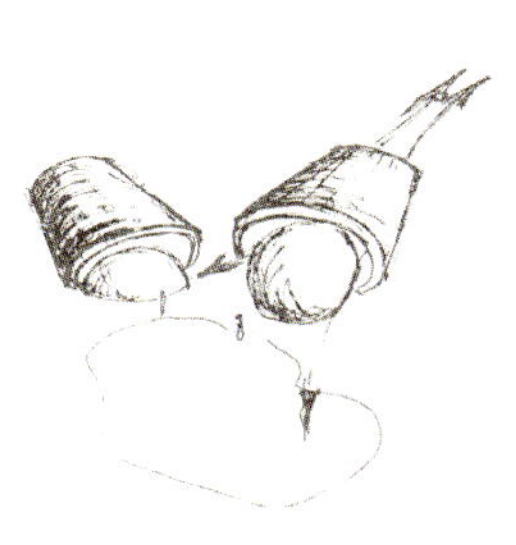

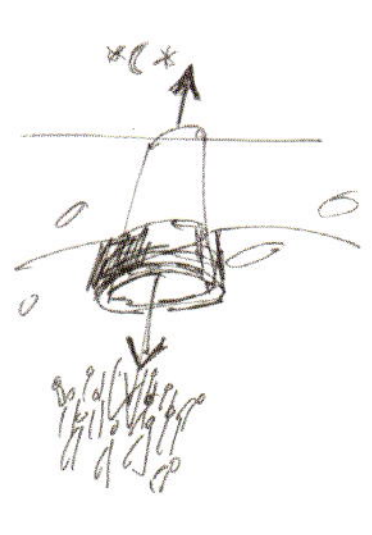

PAVILLON DU JARDIN DES PREMIÈRES-NATIONS

This pavilion, reached by a path through the woods, was built to commemorate the 300th anniversary of the *Grand Paix*, the treaty signed with First Nations peoples in 1701. Its undulating canopy of thin concrete, clad in lead-covered copper, follows the topography of the pathway, and the long lean curve of the structure appears as a screen between the deciduous and coniferous sections of the forest. The pavilion is built partially below grade, so as to further submerge it into the landscape. Materials that were clearly chosen for their durability, such as concrete formed with wood slats, are juxtaposed with natural woods and vertical glass showcases. The effect is at the same time transparent, inviting and poetic.

Architects	**Saucier + Perrotte**
Client	**Jardin botanique de Montréal / Ville de Montréal**
Completed	**2001**
Address	**Jardin botanique de Montréal, 4101 rue Sherbrooke Ouest**
Métro	**Pie-IX**
Access	**see website**

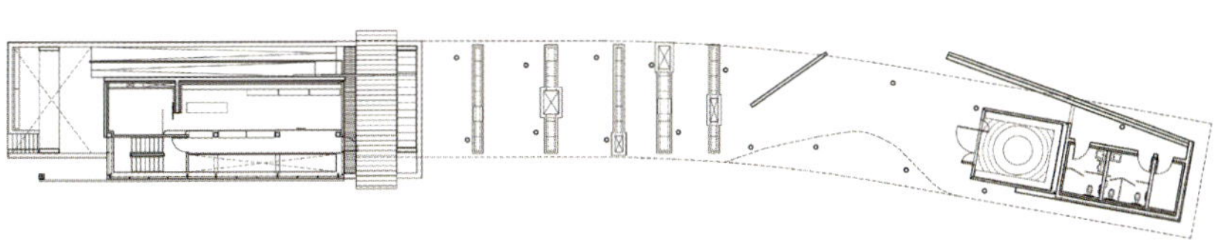

Rachel
Gauthier
Parc La Fontaine
Émile-Duployé
des Érables
Messier
Sherbrooke
D'Iberville
Frontenac
du Havre
Rouen
Parc des Royaux
Larivière
Papineau
Cartier
Dorion
de Bordeaux
De Lorimer
Beaudry
de la Visitation
Panet
Plessis
Métro Frontenac
Ontario
Coupal
Théâtre Espace Libre
Delorme
Usine C
Lalonde
La Fontaine
La Fontaine
Alexandre-DeSève
Champlain
Logan
Parthenais
Fullum
Dufresne
Poupart
Métro Papineau
De Maisonneuve
Métro Beaudry
Sainte-Catherine
René-Lévesque
Notre-Dame
Viger
0
200 metres
2 minutes to walk

STE. MARIE

Ste. Marie is the original name for an industrial neighbourhood known as *Faubourg à m'lasse* from the mid-19th to the mid-20th centuries, where tobacco, textile and food factories were located, as well as housing for the workers. Industry vacated the area in the 1950s. The late-1960s urban renewal scheme put forward by then mayor Jean Drapeau entailed demolition of more than 1000 housing units with the intent of creating a *Cité des ondes*, a whole *quartier* devoted to the telecommunications industry, running from La Fontaine Park to the river. Maison Radio-Canada was built and opened in 1973, but the area around it was razed for parking, and the rest of the scheme was never realized.

The Gay Village is a relatively recent name for the western part of Ste. Marie on Ste. Catherine between St. Hubert and Papineau, where starting from a cluster of restaurants and clubs in the 1990s, the presence of the gay community has revitalized the whole neighbourhood. Every summer since 2011, Claude Cormier's exuberant *Pink Balls* installation has hung over a kilometre-long stretch of Ste. Catherine, "pedestrianized" from St. Hubert to Papineau.

Like many other *quartiers* in the city, Ste. Marie is looking at ways to revitalize. What will be interesting to see is whether that change is driven by big projects like the possible densification of the Maison Radio-Canada site or the borough's own planning proposals.

USINE C

After twenty years of wandering, the avant-garde performance troupe Carbone 14 chose a former jam factory – Usine Raymond – as its permanent home. A tall brick chimney capped with a sculpture by Richard Purdy signals the presence of the cultural complex in the neighbourhood known in the early 20th century as *Faubourg à m'lasse*.

A new theatre space clad in recycled brick was added to the north of the existing structure, which runs east-west on Lalonde, thus defining the circulation along two intersecting axes. A glazed node at this intersection links new construction to old, both horizontally and vertically. This node overlooks an interior courtyard and a spiral stair that leads to offices and the entry to the auditorium. The 450-seat theatre is a large black box that can be reconfigured for different seating formats. The ramp leading to the west entry on Visitation becomes a *passerelle*, which traverses the former boiler room below, now home to a lively café.

Materials are everything here. The contrast between the muscularity of the exposed concrete and the delicacy of glass is executed with a beguiling simplicity.

Architects	**Saucier + Perrotte**
Client	**Carbone 14**
Completed	**1995**
Address	**1345 Rue Lalonde**
Métro	**Beaudry**
Access	**see website**

THÉÂTRE ESPACE LIBRE

A neat solution to a problem common to many small cultural organizations. The theatre company Espace Libre had outgrown the former fire station that had been its home for twenty years and wanted to renovate to provide rehearsal and performance space for itself and two other theatre companies. A very tight budget and a tighter site meant excising part of the building, filling it with a modern box and adding floors below grade and on the roof. Of the original fire station, only the front façade and part of the south façade, the party wall, and the hose tower remain.

The main performance space occupies the whole ground floor, accessible via the original garage doors. Each theatre company has its own rehearsal and office spaces, with separate entry doors; the stairway leading to them is visible through the glazed south façade. The zigzagged curtain wall that wraps around the east face is operable, providing natural ventilation. The fire hall turned theatre is at its best at night, when the light behind the glass façade glows a greeny yellow.

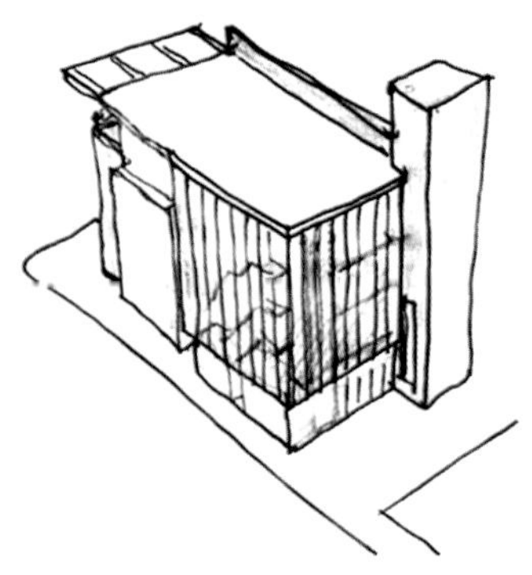

Architects	**Lapointe Magne et Associés**
Client	**Théâtre Espace Libre**
Completed	**2002**
Address	**1845 Rue Fullum**
Métro	**Frontenac**
Access	**exterior only**

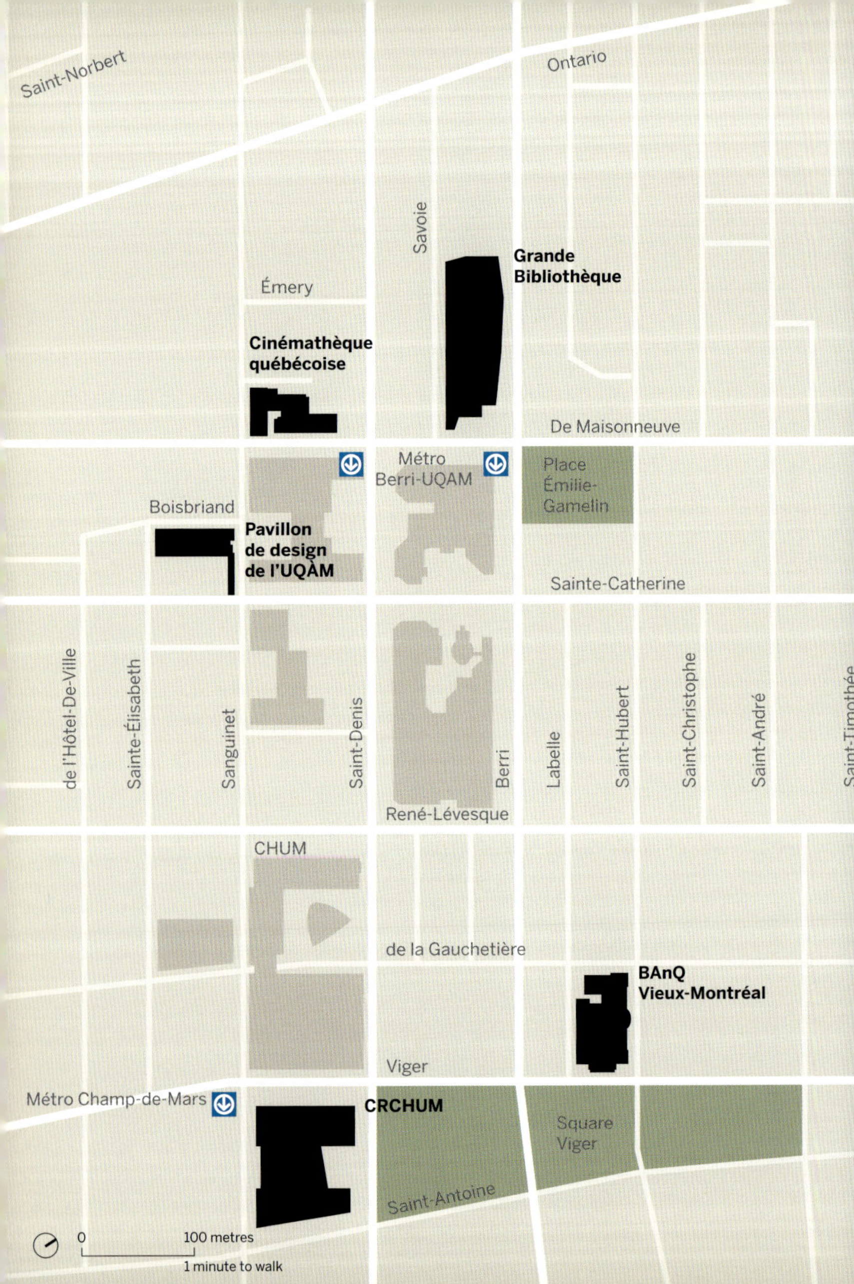
Saint-Norbert
Ontario
Savoie
Grande Bibliothèque
Émery
Cinémathèque québécoise
De Maisonneuve
Métro Berri-UQAM
Place Émilie-Gamelin
Boisbriand
Pavillon de design de l'UQÀM
Sainte-Catherine
de l'Hôtel-De-Ville
Sainte-Élisabeth
Sanguinet
Saint-Denis
Berri
Labelle
Saint-Hubert
Saint-Christophe
Saint-André
Saint-Timothée
René-Lévesque
CHUM
de la Gauchetière
BAnQ Vieux-Montréal
Viger
Métro Champ-de-Mars
CRCHUM
Square Viger
Saint-Antoine
0
100 metres
1 minute to walk

QUARTIER LATIN

For the short twenty-year period between the two world wars, St. Denis was the cultural heart of francophone Montreal. Home to the École des hautes études commerciales and the medical and law faculties of the nascent Université de Montréal, the area attracted theatres and cafés. The Bibliothèque Saint-Sulpice, Montreal's first French-language library, opened here in 1915.

In 1943, the Université de Montréal moved to the north slopes of Mount Royal and the once-elegant greystones emptied out. The Quartier Latin deteriorated badly – revival started only in the 1960s, with quirky stores and restaurants. The creation of the new Université du Québec à Montréal (UQÀM) in 1969 meant the return of people to the neighbourhood but to some rather dire Brutalist concrete buildings anchored to the Berri-UQÀM metro station.

The interior-focused UQÀM buildings made public spaces all the more important. Place Émilie-Gamelin, designed in 1992, never worked as it was intended and was both indeterminate and slightly sketchy. It was given a new green lease on life in 2015, with the creation of community gardens and a farmer's market.

Cultural institutions emblematic of late-20th-century Québec, such as the Cinémathèque and the Grande Bibliothèque, infused the *quartier* with energy and renewed purpose in the 1990s.

The southern edge of the *quartier* has been extraordinarily intensified by the construction of the CHUM (Centre hospitalier de l'Université de Montréal), built next to and on top of the depressed Ville-Marie expressway. The open trench of the expressway itself will be covered over from Mètro Champ-de-Mars to Hôtel-de-ville, and Square Viger, a Victorian square rebuilt in 1981 as its roof, is to be reconfigured.

PAVILLON DE DESIGN DE L'UQÀM

In stark contrast to the massive concrete hulks that the university built in the 1970s, this complex added cachet to the UQÀM urban campus. The Pavillon de design programme included studios, classrooms and offices for the schools of design de l'environnement and graphic design as well as exhibition space for the Centre de design.

The building fronts onto Sanguinet, with a finger stretching down to Ste. Catherine. The main volume extends back from Sanguinet along Boisbriand. Eight storeys high, it is organized around a daylit open core, through which passages cross and stairways mount. This is not a simple building – there are many layers, and the best way to see the building is to start at the top at the tiny roof garden and walk down. The ground floor is the public space, with the Centre de design gallery ideally positioned for access from the street. Like most UQÀM buildings, this pavilion is linked by tunnel to the metro.

The design pavilion is robust and intended for hard use. Materials are industrial – steel mesh, steel checkerplate, exposed concrete – and are employed exuberantly, with careful detailing throughout.

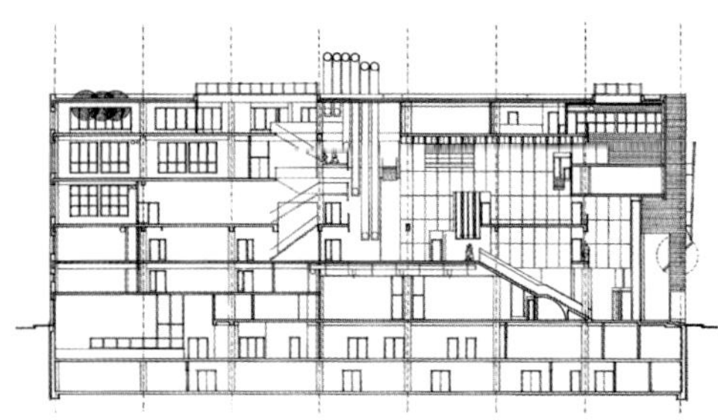

Architects	**Dan S. Hanganu**
Client	**UQÀM**
Completed	**1996**
Address	**1440 Rue Sanguinet**
Métro	**Berri-UQAM**
Access	**university hours**

CINÉMATHÈQUE QUÉBÉCOISE

Reusing two former school buildings on De Maisonneuve – and more importantly, inserting new volumes into the space between the two – gave the Cinémathèque québécoise (an important repository of Québécois films) a presence in the Quartier Latin. The entry, a cube described by the architect as a light-box, sits poised slightly back from the sidewalk and at night seems to extend beyond it into the street. A glass and metal box projects out from the face of the entry cube and serves as a translucent projection screen: people moving across the ramp immediately behind it are suddenly actors onscreen.

To enter the building, the visitor crosses a metal bridge over a narrow gap. Inside, an agora – a balcony of raked seating – cantilevers out at mid-level in the volume of the entry box, allowing visitors to view projections on the screen on the north wall. The palette is deliberately black and white, and the materials are sleek, in contrast to the exposed concrete frame that delineates the boundary between old and new construction.

To the west of the entry, a courtyard leads to a café folded into the heart of the building. A médiathèque below grade is lit by natural light from the courtyard. Exhibition galleries, a small theatre and a video projection room are in the new volume; offices are in the former Jeanne Mance school to the east.

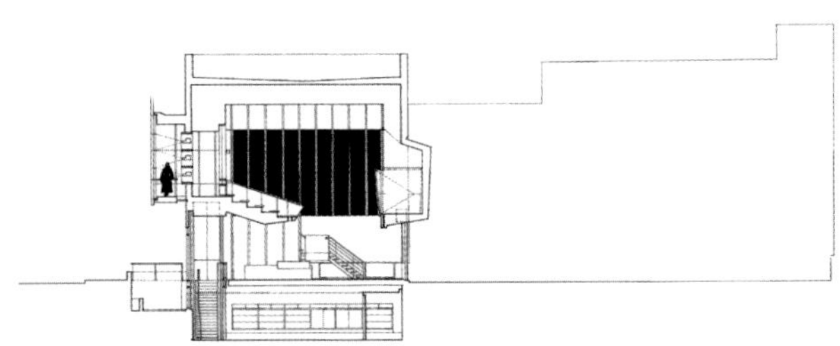

Architects	**Saucier + Perrotte**
Client	**Cinémathèque québécoise**
Completed	**1997**
Address	**355 Boul. De Maisonneuve Est**
Métro	**Berri-UQAM**
Access	**see website**

GRANDE BIBLIOTHÈQUE

Significant both for its architecture and its content, the project for Quebec's new library was subjected to constant scrutiny – from the international architectural competition in 2000 to its inauguration in 2005. Few architects from outside Quebec have been given such major commissions in the last thirty-plus years, and few projects have been as culturally important.

The library is a great long rectangular metal box (33,000 square metres, six storeys high), clad in pale-green ceramic-coated glass tile; it connects both to the street and to the metro one floor below. At street level, there are two main entrances, at either end of a long public passage flooded with natural light.

On the inside, the building is generous and eminently readable. The ease with which one moves up through the central core and around the perimeter is remarkable given the complexity of the programme.

The library's two principal holdings – the lending/reference collection and the *collection Québécoise*, which includes everything ever published in Québec – are contained in two immense and beautiful wood-slatted volumes, one at the centre of the building and the other at the northern end. These *chambres de bois* (inspired by the novelist Anne Hébert) subtly use wood as a backdrop to reading spaces and study carrels.

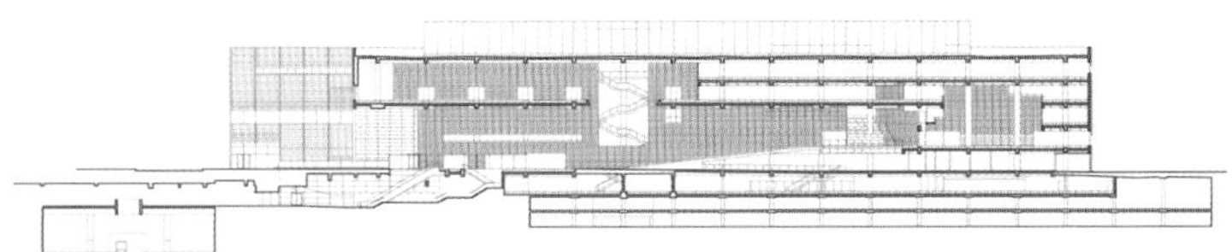

Architects	**Patkau / Croft Pelletier / Menkès Shooner Dagenais**
Client	**Bibliothèque et Archives nationales du Québec**
Completed	**2005**
Address	**475 Boul. De Maisonneuve Est**
Métro	**Berri-UQAM**
Access	**see website**

BAnQ VIEUX-MONTRÉAL

Quebec's cultural history is archived in a network of regional centres and in the Grande Bibliothèque. At the BAnQ Vieux-Montréal, located in a complex of buildings that occupies a city block fronting onto Viger, researchers have access to Montreal documents dating back to the 17th century.

Dan S.Hanganu / Provencher Roy won the competition organized in 1997 to reuse and add onto four existing buildings on the site, including the 1911 École des hautes études commerciales building and the 1870 Maison Jodoin.

There is a sense of revelation as the visitor moves from the imposing entry lobby up the stairs and into the bold six-storey glazed atrium at the core. On the north side of the atrium, the original doors now float in a mullionless wall of glass, and beyond, an interior courtyard leads to the consultation room. This space for researchers is housed in the wonderful cast-iron fantasy of the former 1916 *Musée industriel et commercial*. Here, as everywhere in this project, the attitude of combining new with old is straightforward – as demonstrated by the circular stair that has been inserted with clarity and assurance.

Not to be overlooked is the new storage structure, seen best from Labelle – a grey zinc box with an elegant metal trellis for vines.

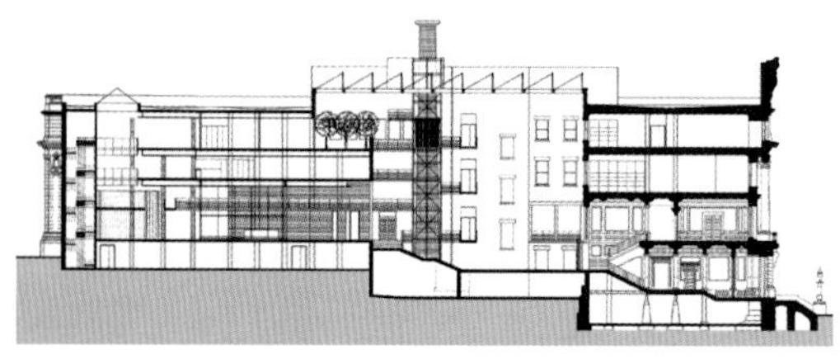

Architects	**Dan S. Hanganu / Provencher Roy et Associés**
Client	**Société immobilière du Québec**
Completed	**1999**
Address	**535 Av. Viger Est**
Métro	**Champ-de-Mars**
Access	**interior lobby only – see website**

CENTRE DE RECHERCHE DU CHUM

Montreal is home to two "super-hospitals," two massive construction projects that have each seen the consolidation of several hospitals on single sites. The CHUM (Centre hospitalier de l'Université de Montréal), a three-phase project built over ten years on one of the tightest sites imaginable at the southern edge of the Quartier Latin, brings together three hospitals and creates a new research centre to serve the new entity.

The Centre de recherche is the first phase, built as a PPP (private-public partnership) separate from the hospital proper. The fifteen-storey tower on Viger sits on top of the metro line, and the second six-storey pavilion is immediately to the south of the Ville-Marie expressway; the two are linked by a *passerelle*. The volumes of the research centre act as the transition between Old Montreal and the much taller hospital across the street that will occupy the entire block from Viger to René-Lévesque, between Sanguinet and St. Denis. The tunnel connecting the whole project to the metro station runs through the Viger tower.

The main entry to the research centre on St. Denis is glazed and open, the space inside serving both as lobby and clinical reception area – a curious ungenerous solution, despite the presence of some first-rate Québécois contemporary art. The sombre exterior cladding was chosen to align the centre with the hospital, but the need to have opaque walls and to protect many of the labs from natural light has meant the façade is somewhat forbidding. The western façade immediately opposite the entrance to the Champ-de-Mars metro would have benefited from a more public face.

The second phase of the project, the hospital, will be complete in 2016 and the administrative buildings in 2020.

Architects	**NFOE / Menkès Shooner Dagenais LeTourneux / Jodoin Lamarre Pratte / Lemay / Parkin**
Landscape architect	**NIPpaysage**
Client	**Accès Recherche CHUM**
Completed	**2013**
Address	**900 Rue Saint-Denis**
Métro	**Champ-de-Mars**
Access	**exterior only**

Fairmount
Laurier
Métro Laurier
Édouard-Charles
Saint-Joseph
Théâtre Espace Go
Les Quatre Arbres
Villeneuve
Jeanne-Mance
de l'Esplanade
Pontiac
Resther
Boyer
du Mont-Royal
Métro Mont-Royal
Maison Coloniale
Marie-Anne
Pavot rouge
Parc Mont-Royal
Parc Jeanne-Mance
À l'ombre de Paris
Rachel
Box House
Saint-Laurent
Saint-Dominique
Coloniale
De Bullion
de l'Hôtel-de-Ville
Laval
Henri-Julien
Drolet
Saint-Denis
du Parc
Duluth
Bagg
Napoléon
Roy
Tower House
des Pins
Rivard
Berri
De Chateaubriand
Saint-Hubert
Saint-Christophe
Saint-André
de Mentana
du Parc La Fontaine
Théâtre de Quat'sous
Square Saint-Louis
Institut de tourisme et d'hôtellerie du Québec
Prince-Arthur
Métro Sherbrooke
University
Durocher
Hutchison
Jeanne-Mance
Sainte-Famille
Saint-Urbain
Milton
Sherbrooke
Labrecque
Amherst
Saint-Norbert
Ontario
Sanguinet
Savoie
Clark
Saint-Timothée
Président-Kennedy
Métro Place-des-Arts
Métro Saint-Laurent
Métro Berri-UQAM
De Maisonneu
0
200 metres
2 minutes to walk

PLATEAU MONT-ROYAL

The Plateau is a densely built neighbourhood of rowhouses, an *enfilade* of curved staircases that extends north from Sherbrooke to the railway tracks at Van Horne, east to Frontenac and west to the mountain. Built almost entirely in the boom period from 1890 to 1930 – initially to house those who worked in the quarries at the Plateau's northern edge – the area became Montreal's hottest neighbourhood in the late 20th century. The ability to walk out the door and into a restaurant in less than a minute continues to make this a desirable place to live, but the cost of renting a flat (Montreal still has the highest proportion of rental housing in North America) or buying a condo has driven many young Montrealers to *quartiers* like Rosemont.

St. Laurent Blvd. was often the first home to immigrants arriving in the port of Montreal, and the street's character has always reflected that. Geographically, "the Main" divides the city into east and west; traditionally, it was the border between French and English neighbourhoods.

Mont-Royal slices through the *quartier* leading to the mountain and is the dividing line between the four original villages that were amalgamated to make up the Plateau. The street has been revitalized since the 1990s, principally through the efforts of merchants.

There is very little green space or public space in this area of the city. Square St. Louis, an elegant 1879 residential square, and La Fontaine Park, at the southern edge, are welcome exceptions.

MAISON COLONIALE

A house that stands apart from all others. Jacques Rousseau's personal exploration of the city and of architecture – how a house embodies both a city's past and the moment at which it is built – takes form in the house he built for himself on the *tête d'ilôt* of the block formed by Coloniale and De Bullion on Marie-Anne. Its twin, square concrete towers and the courtyard between them are a play on the idea of inside-outside; its four floors move up from public to private. In fact, the house was originally intended as studio, office, exhibition space – and home.

In the interior, the floorplates are not continuously connected to the walls, and partitions are limited to cubicles where needed. In the summer, garage doors at the first-floor level open to the outside at either end of the connecting bridge.

Execution is not perfect. There is an unfinished quality to the construction that has not always served the house well, but much is forgiven, in light of the *beau geste*.

Architect	**Jacques Rousseau**
Client	**private**
Completed	**1990**
Address	**4333 Av. Coloniale**
Métro	**Mont-Royal**
Access	**exterior only**

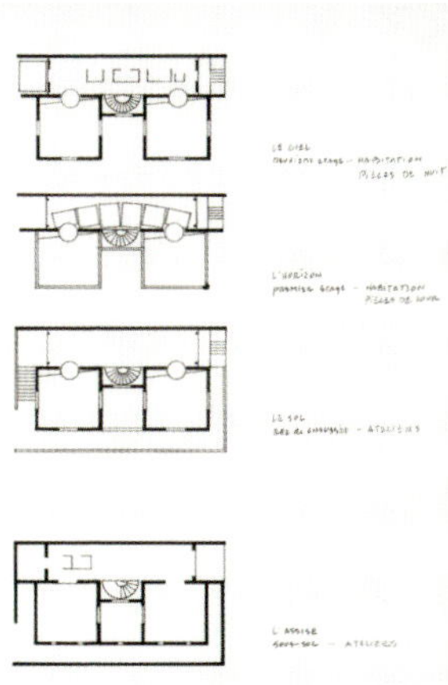

LE CIEL
deuxième étage – HABITATION
PIÈCES DE NUIT
L'HORIZON
premier étage – HABITATION
PIÈCES DE JOUR
LE SOL
rez-de-chaussée – ATELIERS
L'ASSISE
sous-sol – ATELIERS

HOUSES AND HOUSING ON THE PLATEAU

The Montreal triplex – a three-storey rowhouse with an exterior staircase – is a strong housing type that has created a robust streetscape in many *quartiers*. The best new domestic architecture in the Plateau integrates without mimicry; it satisfies the Plateau-Mont-Royal borough's requirements to respect the city's built heritage, while injecting new energy into the neighbourhood.

Tower House is actually two towers with two units each, covering ninety per cent of its corner lot. The insertion of the tiny courtyard allows for large corner windows in each unit: the bridge spanning the courtyard at the third-storey level forms part of the fire escape.

Box House is remarkable because it sits at the intersection of a lane and an alley, so it is quite literally in the middle of the street. Described by the architects as "a box with metal appendages," the house stacks living space above studio, with windows carefully sliced to privilege the view to Mount Royal.

Tower House
3776-82 Av. Laval

Architects **BUILD**
Completed **1997**
Métro **Sherbrooke**

Box House
4056 Rue Saint-Christophe

Architects **BUILD**
Completed **1999**
Métro **Mont-Royal**

Pavot rouge
4274 Rue Saint-Christophe

Architects **YH2**
Completed **2007**
Métro **Mont-Royal**

Pavot Rouge is located on the same alley. This small (ninety-eight square metres) insertion is built on top of an existing garage, wrapped in a glorious orange-red ceramic-glazed brick and topped off by a green roof.

À l'ombre de Paris was built on a vacant lot that stayed that way for a long time because the seven-storey Paris Star building (formerly a textile factory), on the west side of Coloniale, blocked all available light. A duplex – in this case, a house and studio – is built entirely around a large square lightwell at the core. The exterior, of dark-grey block, is discreet, with its small-scale entry and recessed garage door behind a bright-yellow gate.

Les Quatre Arbres is a small twenty-unit project that densifies inside an existing block. Entry through a wood-clad *porte-cochère* leads to a European-feeling courtyard with four orange spiral staircases that rise like trees against the white three-storey backdrop.

À l'ombre de Paris

4227-29 Rue Coloniale

Architects **YH2**
Completed **2001**
Métro **Mont-Royal**

Les Quatre Arbres

4878 Rue Henri-Julien

Architects **Boutros + Pratte**
Completed **2010**
Métro **Laurier**

INSTITUT DE TOURISME ET D'HÔTELLERIE DU QUÉBEC

For the first time in 1974, the Société d'architecture de Montréal – in what was to become a Save Montreal annual tradition – awarded Oranges and Lemons to celebrate the best and worst projects built in the preceding year. The very first Lemon went to the original incarnation of the ITHQ, a 1970 Brutalist eleven-storey tower on a concrete podium entirely out of scale with the neighbourhood.

Thirty years later, the much-maligned building housing the province's hotel and tourism school was completely renovated. A new double skin was wrapped around the structure, giving it a new face and at the same time preheating the air brought into the building. The design focus has been on the elevations – each elevation on the tower is different from the others. On de Rigaud and de Malines there are balconies for the hotel rooms; on the St. Denis façade, the glazing is saw-toothed green and yellow. Fritted glazing across the full width of the podium on St. Denis announces the ITHQ's presence; this side has been opened up at the sidewalk level and glazed, allowing passersby to see into the restaurant and lobby.

Architects	**Lapointe Magne et Associés / Aedifica**
Client	**Société immobilière du Québec**
Completed	**2005**
Address	**3535 Rue Saint-Denis**
Métro	**Sherbrooke**
Access	**interior – lobby areas only**

THÉÂTRE DE QUAT'SOUS

At Av. des Pins and Coloniale, Théâtre de Quat'Sous sits squarely on the street corner and looks out to the Plateau in both directions, taking its place without pushing its way in. The outwardly visible clue to the story of the place is the black silhouette of a man sitting on top of a ladder etched in the glazing of the fourth storey. This homage to Paul Buissonneau, director of the Théâtre de Quat'Sous for almost thirty-five years, speaks to the deep history of the theatre on this site.

Éric Gauthier of FABG faced up to the challenge of having the new theatre speak to the memories embedded in the site by the previous theatre without becoming maudlin. He talks about "mapping" the past onto the new volumes, onto new materials. Marble pieces are reincorporated into a floor, and theatre seats are upholstered in the original red colour – but the feeling is crisp and contemporary.

Glass is used to the maximum – it is transparent and reflective at the same time. The glass panel installation by Hal Ingberg on the rooftop terrace contributes to the sense of being outside but contained.

Théâtre de Quat'Sous succeeds at both evoking the memory of the original theatre and meeting contemporary theatre requirements with grace and élan.

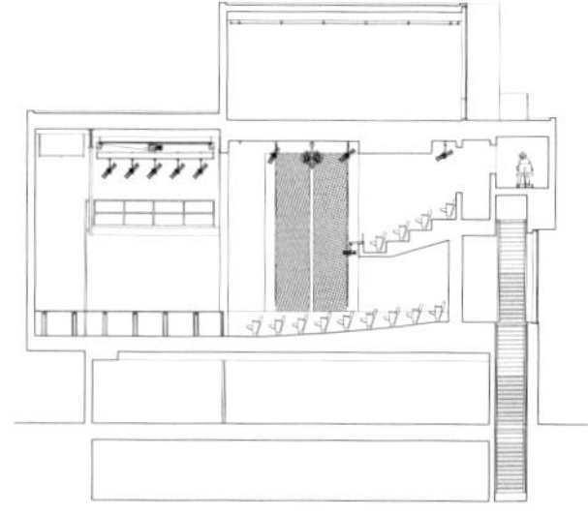

Architects	**FABG**
Client	**Théâtre de Quat'sous**
Completed	**2009**
Address	**100 Av. des Pins Ouest**
Métro	**Sherbrooke**
Access	**see website**

THÉÂTRE ESPACE GO

In 1994, the Espace Go theatre company elected to build a new venue on a vacant lot on a relatively quiet stretch of St. Laurent, rather than reuse an existing building, as did many other small companies at the time. This crisp and collected building inserted itself gracefully into the streetscape and looks as if it has always been there.

Sections of Indiana-limestone clapboard bracket the full-height glazed opening that reveals the foyer, lobby and bar at ground level and offices above. Looking in from the sidewalk, the arcade of thin structural columns and the poetry-etched glass create a certain distance between pedestrian and theatregoer. Once inside, the impression is reversed and the sidewalk feels like part of the foyer.

The three-storey-high theatre space is completely flexible and seats about 250 people, depending on the configuration for the particular production. A rehearsal space contiguous to the main space opens onto Clark, one street to the west. Atypically, there is no laneway in this block, and access to the truck dock is through a *porte-cochère* on the St. Laurent façade.

Architects	**Blouin Faucher Aubertin Brodeur Gauthier**
Client	**Théâtre Espace Go**
Completed	**1995**
Address	**4890 Boul. St-Laurent**
Métro	**Laurier**
Access	**see website**

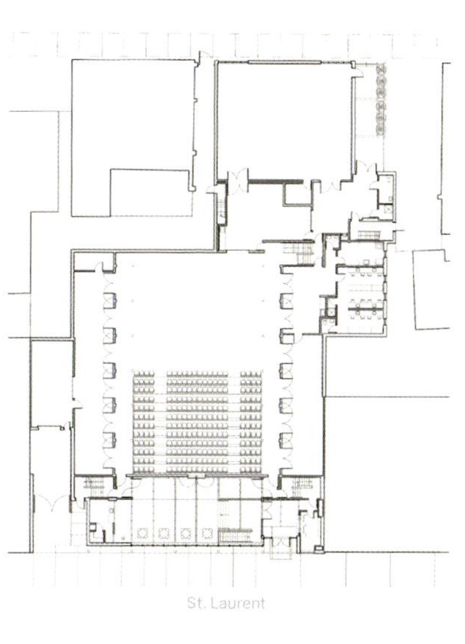
St. Laurent

Métro Parc
Métro De Castelnau
Jean-Talon
Métro Jean-Talon
Marché Jean-Talon
Mozart
Bélanger
Marconi
Alexandra
Waverly
Parc Mozart
Beaumont
Saint-Zotique
Saint-Urbain
Clark
Mile Ex
Saint-Zotique
Beaubien
Little Italy
Métro Beaubien
Beaubien
Van Horne
Saint-Laurent
Saint-Dominique
Casgrain
De Gaspé
Alma
Henri-Julien
Drolet
Saint-Denis
Saint-Vallier
De Chateaubriand
Saint-Hubert
Saint-André
Boyer
Bellechasse
du Parc
Jeanne-Mance
de l'Esplanade
Waverly
Bernard
Bibliothèque Marc-Favreau
Rosemont
Métro Rosemont
Un toit pour tous
Le Coteau vert
des Carrières
Saint-Viateur
Saint-Grégoire
0
200 metres
2 minutes to walk

ROSEMONT / LA PETITE-PATRIE

Rosemont's origins are tied to the quarries, the source of the grey limestone that is the base material for Montreal. The traces of this first industry are slight: the sinuous route of rue des Carrières or the presence of large green spaces that were once quarries, like Parc Père Marquette. The industry that determined its development, however, was the railways. Canadian Pacific's rail line was built in the 1890s, and in 1904, the vast nine-hectare Angus Shops opened, employing more than three thousand people from the outset. The shops closed completely in 1992 and the massive complex has now become the Technopole Angus, an interesting mix of commercial and residential uses.

The western sector of Rosemont was only given the name of La Petite-Patrie in the 1980s, after a novel by Claude Jasmin that recounted his childhood in the neighbourhood. Just as the Rosemont *quartier* was made up of a collection of villages and parishes at the start of the 20th century, La Petite-Patrie is itself made up of a series of "*micro-quartiers*" – Little Italy, Secteur Bellechasse, the area around Jean-Talon market, Mile Ex.

The remaking of La Petite-Patrie has focused on the reuse of the municipal yards along Rosemont and the creation of a new node whose pivot point is the metro station. The Marc Favreau library – including new public green spaces – and residential construction that includes building on top of the metro station itself have created a light in the window, a signal of the revitalization of the area.

BIBLIOTHÈQUE MARC-FAVREAU

The result of an architectural competition in 2009, this Japanese lantern of a library sits with utter confidence on the corner of Rosemont and St. Vallier. Built on what were Rosemont's municipal yards, the project integrates an enfilade of 1930s Art Deco buildings to the east – "Construction" and "Purchases" written in the stone lintels above the doors attest to their original use.

The library is a series of beautifully turned volumes clad in etched glass that face the Rosemont metro station to the west and in cross-braced walls that embrace a new park to the south. Light dances across the corner at night, with the work *Urba Morphic–Volume 1* by the Société des arts technologiques (artist Louis-Phillippe St. Arnault) paying homage to the actor Marc Favreau. A lover of language, Favreau's character Sol appears on the Morris column at the entryway. The park is named after Luc Durand, the actor who appeared with Favreau in the 1960s television show *Sol et Gobelet*.

The interior of the library is a series of defined spaces with distinct uses – the children's library is on the ground floor and the storytelling area is immediately inside the front door – skillfully knit together. There is a multiplicity of materials, but they serve to define; details like the railings on the stairs are completely assured.

Architects	**Dan S. Hanganu**
Client	**Arrondissement Rosemont–La Petite-Patrie**
Completed	**2013**
Address	**500 Boul. Rosemont**
Métro	**Rosemont**
Access	**see website**

500
Bibliothèque
Marc-Favreau

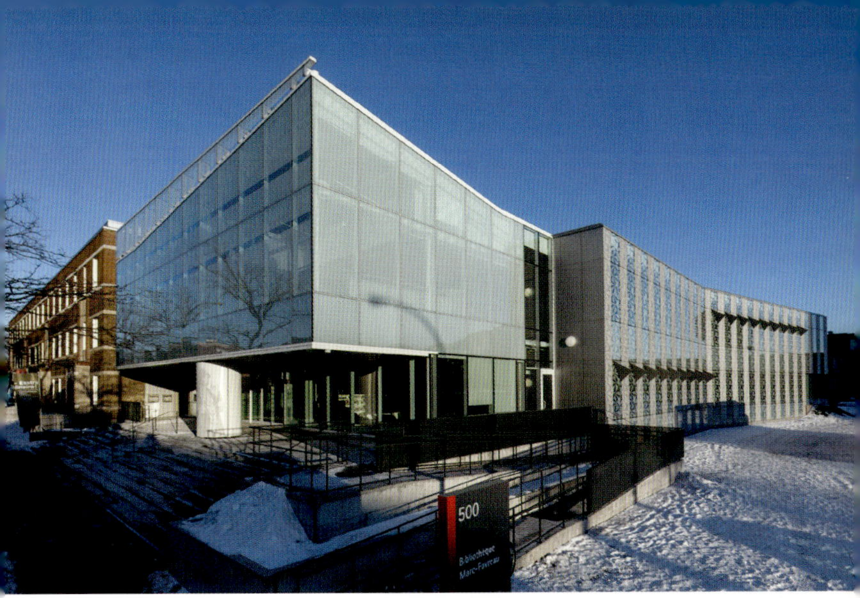

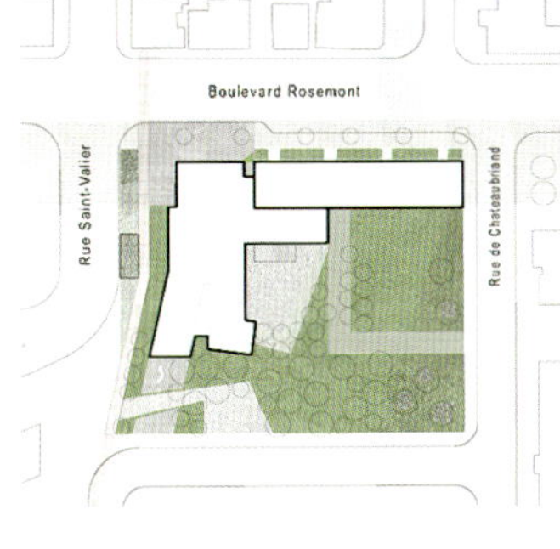

Boulevard Rosemont
Rue Saint-Vallier
Rue de Chateaubriand

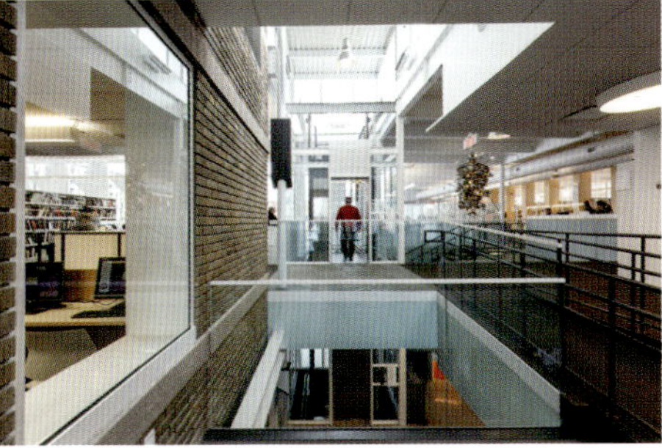

LE COTEAU VERT AND UN TOIT POUR TOUS

Sustainable housing construction is as much about the process as it is about the built form – and involvement requires commitment to a neighbourhood. In this case, the neighbourhood is both the older *quartier* of Rosemont and the newer node created around the library and the metro station.

The housing co-op *Le Coteau vert* for families and the not-for-profit *Un toit pour tous* for small households comprise 155 units built on the decontaminated former Rosemont–La Petite-Patrie municipal workshop site. A three-storey wood structure divided into eight buildings sited around a semi-private courtyard, the project features straightforward strategies, such as orienting the buildings to optimize natural light and using sustainable materials like torrefied wood, but also includes horizontal geothermic heating and a series of water management systems.

But the pleasure in the project lies in the experience of walking through the *porte-cochère* into the courtyard and seeing all the details that make it work. Clotheslines, garden sheds and a scale that is just right make this more a community than a project.

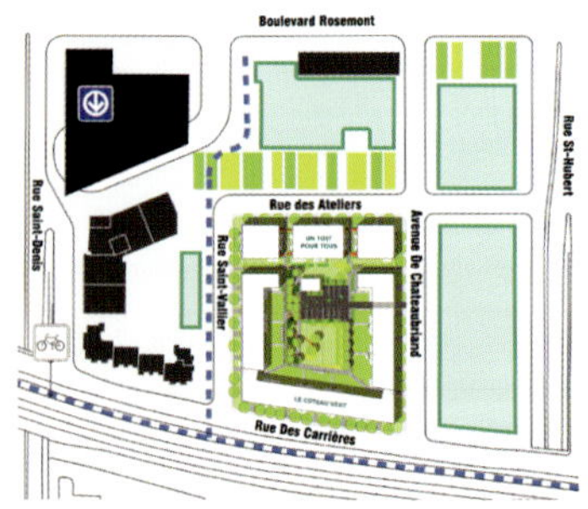

Architects	**L'OEUF**
Landscape architect	**NIPpaysage**
Client	**Coop Le Coteau vert / GRT Bâtir son quartier / OBNL Un toit pour tous**
Completed	**2010**
Address	**between Chateaubriand and Saint-Valliers, from des Ateliers to des Carrières**
Métro	**Rosemont**
Access	**exterior only**

MILE EX

Mile Ex is a recent name for a neighbourhood known to many Montrealers as Marconi/Alexandra, called Mile Ex as a hybrid of Mile End to the south and Parc Ex(tension) to the north. Defined by the Canadian Pacific Railway tracks to the south and Jean Talon to the north, the street pattern is a disjointed hodgepodge relative to the long narrow grid that is typically Montreal. Little Italy ends at St. Laurent, and walking west on Mozart past Clark, one immediately senses one is in a different neighbourhood.

It's the absolute mix that makes it interesting. Home since the 19th century to small industries like mechanic shops, a cardboard box factory and carpet cleaners, the neighbourhood is interspersed with clusters of duplexes and triplexes, tiny owner-built houses and a veritable forest of telephone poles. In the late 1990s, as industries left, the area began to attract architects who could be inventive in this area on the margins. They designed their own homes and opened offices here.

It was inevitable that there would be some zoning intervention by the borough – here conversion of industrial to residential has been limited, encouraging reuse of industrial space as artist studios and offices, maintaining the essential mix. There are insertions and recycled buildings sprinkled on every street in Mile Ex. They have all been built since 2000, and the materiality alone is intriguing. Rather than pinpoint any or all of them, this map invites you to take the metro to De Castelnau and go for a walk.

Ogilvy
Gare Jean-Talon
De Castelnau
Métro De Castelnau
Métro Parc
Jean-Talon
Marconi
Alexandra
Waverly
Saint-Urbain
Mozart
Parc Mozart
Beaumont
Bélanger
Dante
Saint-Zotique
Mile Ex
Hutchison
du Parc
Jeanne-Mance
de l'Esplanade
Waverly
Saint-Urbain
Clark
Beaubien
Van Horne
Saint-Laurent
Saint-Dominique
Casgrain
De Gaspé
Bellechasse
0
100 metres
1 minute to walk

de Louvain
Stade de soccer de Montréal
de Louvain
Legendre
Émile-Journault
Émile-Journault
Christophe-Colomb
Papineau
Complexe environnemental de Saint-Michel
Saint-Michel
Parc Jean-Rivard
Deville
Jacques-Casault
Jean-Rivard
Cirque du Soleil
115 Studios – Cirque du Soleil
Autoroute métropolitaine
des Regrattiers
TOHU
École nationale de cirque
Michel-Jurdant
Crémazie
Paul-Boutet
2e Avenue
Jarry
Henri-Brien
Parc Villeray
Tillemont
Villeray
Chambord
Fabre
De Lorimier
1re Avenue
L.-O.-David
Everett
Métro Saint-Michel
0
200 metres
2 minutes to walk
Métro Fabre
Jean-Talon
Métro D'Iberville

ST. MICHEL

St. Michel was a village and still home to farmers until the end of the Second World War, though the dominant industry was the quarries, established as early as the 1750s. By the 1950s, the Miron and Francon quarries were immense, producing gravel and sand. Miron's massive cement factory fed the building boom in downtown Montreal and the 1959 construction of the St. Lawrence Seaway, but its tall chimneys made the neighbourhood a hot spot of pollution. Closed in 1968, the Miron quarry became a waste-disposal site, which was itself closed in 2000 and converted to the Complexe environnemental de Saint-Michel.

Cirque du Soleil's 1995 decision to build its headquarters on the edge of the Miron quarry – and the subsequent construction of an amazing collection of buildings dedicated to the circus arts – has helped to revitalize St. Michel. However, the potential for the Cité des arts du cirque to be a truly cohesive campus remains unrealized.

On the west edge of the former quarry, a massive soccer stadium completed in 2015 speaks to the preoccupation of Montreal's boroughs with the design and construction of sports facilities. The stadium is one component of a long-term plan for the environmental complex; the central core of the park will open partially in 2017.

CIRQUE DU SOLEIL

Cirque du Soleil is the Quebec troupe that grew from a big-top in Montreal's Old Port in the 1980s to shows that tour the world and permanent installations in Las Vegas and Orlando. This international headquarters houses rehearsal space as well as costume and prop studios for all Cirque productions.

The choice of site – it's built on the southern edge of the now-closed Miron quarry/dump – was seen as adventurous in the mid-1990s. Conceived from the outset as an integral part of the adjacent Complexe environnemental de Saint-Michel, Hanganu's building was a strong statement in a marginal landscape.

Built as a "work in progress" (its first extension was undertaken during the original construction), the structure has since been enlarged twice by FABG. Clad in corrugated metal siding, it is now industrial in scale as well as materials. The most interesting façade is the fragmented north side that overlooks the Place du Chapiteau and the Miron quarry beyond; that façade and the whimsical steel-mesh-draped main entry are the strongest exterior evidence of Hanganu's playfulness.

Inside the building (visitors can enter only as far as the lobby), a massive skylit corridor is an interior street over which catwalks and balconies project. Here, performers, artisans and management are brought into constant contact with one another.

Architects	**Dan S. Hanganu (original building) / FABG (additions)**
Client	**Cirque du Soleil**
Completed	**1997 (original building), 2000 and 2007 (additions)**
Address	**8400 2e Avenue**
Métro	**D'Iberville (+ bus 94 nord)**
Access	**exterior and lobby only**

115 STUDIOS – CIRQUE DU SOLEIL

This series of studios houses artists and performers who come to train with the Cirque du Soleil before joining one of its many productions. In reality, there are two buildings: a pile of "stacked containers" that faces the Cirque du Soleil headquarters across the street and a low three-storey block on rue Jean-Rivard, which is more in scale with the housing immediately to the east. The starkness of the low block, while enlivened by an alternating window pattern, is almost too modest next to the exuberance of the containers. Both volumes are clad in copper-coloured metal panels that radiate warmth.

Some studios can be combined to create larger spaces; all have access to communal areas, including a fitness room, an internet café and living rooms. The studios in the cube of containers are built around a glazed central atrium – light floods in from above.

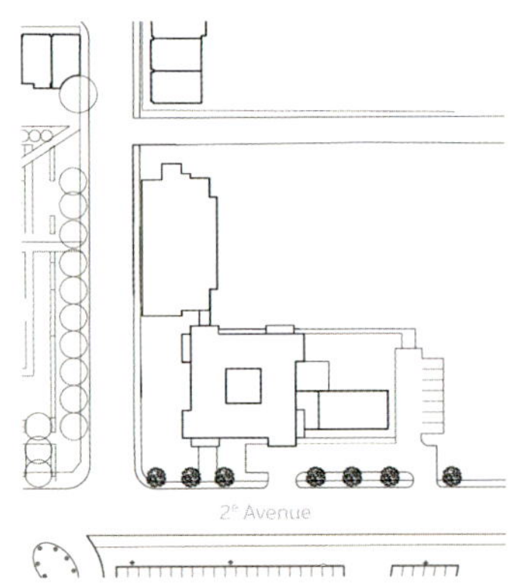

Architects	**FABG**
Client	**Cirque du Soleil**
Completed	**2004**
Address	**8333 2e Avenue**
Métro	**D'Iberville (+ bus 94 nord)**
Access	**exterior only**

ÉCOLE NATIONALE DE CIRQUE

The École nationale de cirque sits like a tall ship becalmed in the somewhat bleak landscape of the Cité des arts du cirque. In this way, it fulfils its original purpose – as a signpost for the precinct from the Metropolitan expressway.

A well-composed object, its height is a function of the architects' decision to stack the two eleven-metre-high gymnasia required for trapeze and aerial work. Extensive glazing provides natural light for the gyms, diffused by sun shades on the sloped south face and by translucent glass on the west. Performance spaces are in the centre, while classrooms and offices are on the perimeter of the building.

The landscaped sculpture terrace at the entry designed by NIP paysage is appropriately flippant – this is a circus school – but the semi-submerged space below looks strangely like a basement apartment.

Architects	**Lapointe Magne et associés**
Landscape architects	**NIPpaysage**
Client	**École nationale de cirque**
Completed	**2003**
Address	**8181 2e Avenue**
Métro	**D'Iberville (+ bus 94 nord)**
Access	**exterior only**

TOHU

As the public face of the Cité des arts du cirque, TOHU is a performance space, a community cultural centre and a gateway to the Complexe environnemental de Saint-Michel. The name comes from *tohu-bohu*, meaning hurly-burly or confusion – the chaos that precedes renewal. Built to be an exemplar of sustainability, TOHU is a worthy solution to a demanding programme.

The rusty-orange-coloured cylindrical theatre dominates the structure. Built of pre-cast, self-load-bearing concrete panels, it is a permanent big top for circus presentations. An exhibition area and offices for the not-for-profit organization that manages TOHU occupy a low wing tangential to the circular hall. The back-of-house and artists' entrance are on the opposite, expressway, side of the theatre.

The most innovative aspects of this project are not immediately apparent, including a passive geothermic / low-velocity diffusion heating and ventilation system that reduces energy use by seventy per cent, relative to a conventional installation. Radiant in-floor heating in the concrete slabs uses water warmed by waste heat from the adjacent biogas plant. A particularly theatrical gesture in the main lobby is a glass panel inset into the floor, which allows a look at the "ice box" below – a natural cooling system.

Architects **Schème / Jacques Plante / Jodoin Lamarre Pratte et Associés**
Client **TOHU, La Cité des arts du cirque**
Completed **2004**
Address **2345 Jarry est (entry via des Regrattiers)**
Métro **D'Iberville (+ bus 94 nord)**
Access **see website**

STADE DE SOCCER DE MONTRÉAL

The sheer size of this building takes one by surprise. The very particular conditions of the site, a long strip of land on the western edge of the former Miron quarry, allow it to be this size – perhaps even demand it – but approaching it via Papineau, one is still startled by the great prow of the roof extending to the south.

The result of an architectural competition in 2011, the soccer stadium is part of a long-term plan for the Complexe environnemental de Saint-Michel, along with the Taz skate park to the south, by architect Pierre Thibault. There are two soccer pitches, one interior and one exterior.

Viewed from the pitch to the north, the roof is folded to meet the earth, strata-like in appearance. But on the south side, the entirely glazed façade rises up and is crowned by a roof whose structure is made up of a honeycomb of massive laminated wood beams of extraordinary depth – some as tall as four metres. The innovative wood structure is undoubtedly the wow factor of this building, but the other material is the light. Full-height glazing on the quarry side allows light to pour in and provides a broad-scale view of the quarry turned park.

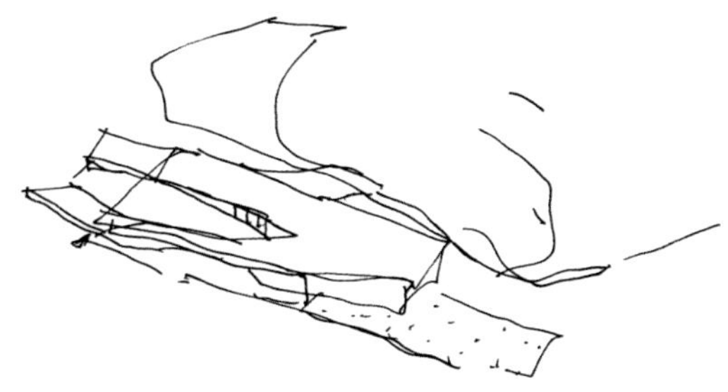

Architects	**Saucier + Perrotte / Hughes Condon Marler**
Client	**Ville de Montréal**
Completed	**2015**
Address	**9235 Av. Papineau**
Métro	**Fabre (+ bus 45)**
Access	**see website**

Bates
Université de Montréal site Outremont
Goyer
Barclay
Ducharme
Les projets Europa, phase IV
Hudson
Van Horne
Métro Outremont
Darlington
Wilderton
De Vimy
Lajoie
Rockland
Davaar
McEachran
Dollard
Stuart
Wiseman
Outremont
Champagneur
Bloomfield
De L'Épée
Querbes
Pavillon de la Faculté de l'aménagement
Côte-Sainte-Catherine
Bernard
HEC Montréal
Willowdale
Édouard-Montpetit
Saint-Viateur
Lacombe
Métro Université-de-Montréal
Métro Édouard-Montpetit
Chemin de la Tour
Université de Montréal
Pavillon J.-Armand-Bombardier
Mont-Royal
Maplewood
Chemin de Polytechnique
Cimetière Notre-Dame-des-Neiges
Cimetière Mont-Royal
Remembrance
Parc du Mont-Royal
0
400 metres
4 minutes to walk
Docteur Penfield

UNIVERSITÉ DE MONTRÉAL / OUTREMONT

Université de Montréal inaugurated its new campus on the north side of Mount Royal in 1943, having moved from the Quartier Latin, the area around St. Denis and Ste. Catherine. The site, given to the university by the City of Montreal, bordered the community of Côte-des-Neiges. Predominantly rural until the First World War, the area developed rapidly in the 1920s, in part because of the tramways and in part because of the start of construction of St. Joseph's Oratory (completed only in 1955) and other institutions, such as Collège Jean-de-Brébeuf. Today, Côte-des-Neiges is home to a multiplicity of hospitals and schools.

The Université de Montréal campus and its principal building are the work of renowned Montreal architect Ernest Cormier. The central pavilion is a graceful example of the monumentality that characterized the 1930s in other parts of the world – less common in Montreal because there was so little built during the Depression. Indeed, construction of the central pavilion with its now-iconic tower started in 1928 but was stopped entirely for more than ten years. Subsequent construction from the 1960s to the 1990s densified the campus, and direct links to a metro station made it more accessible.

Outremont is an affluent, primarily residential community with generous street widths, mature trees and a network of parks established in the 1910s with the deliberate intention of maintaining its garden city character. It is undergoing significant change as the Université de Montréal builds an entirely new campus on reclaimed railway yards at its northern edge. With the railway line relocated to the north, the intent is to extend Outremont's street grid and build a new science node.

PAVILLON DE LA FACULTÉ DE L'AMÉNAGEMENT

In 1994, Université de Montréal mounted an architectural competition to enlarge and renovate the former convent that housed the Faculté de l'aménagement (home to architecture, interior design, urban planning and industrial design), to create a new landscaped public space and integrate the whole into the fabric of the university campus. Saucier + Perrotte's winning solution positioned a rectangular volume for studios to intersect with the original building. However, the signature piece of the project is the dark-red four-hundred-seat auditorium, inserted into the void created by removing the chapel from the existing building. A generous entry lobby, complete with grand staircase, functions as crush space for the auditorium and, more importantly, as part of the public life of the building.

On the Côte Ste. Catherine façade, a Cor-Ten panel was superimposed on the existing yellow brick in a curiously unsuccessful gesture devised to signal the presence of the auditorium. On the campus side, the new construction is wrapped in a grate-like curtain wall pierced by a bridge, which serves as the principal access to the building. Once inside, the bridge traverses an interior courtyard space and exhibition gallery below.

Studios in the new block were conceived and built as entirely open space, partly in the Bauhaus tradition, partly as reaction to the tightly crammed layout of the existing convent building.

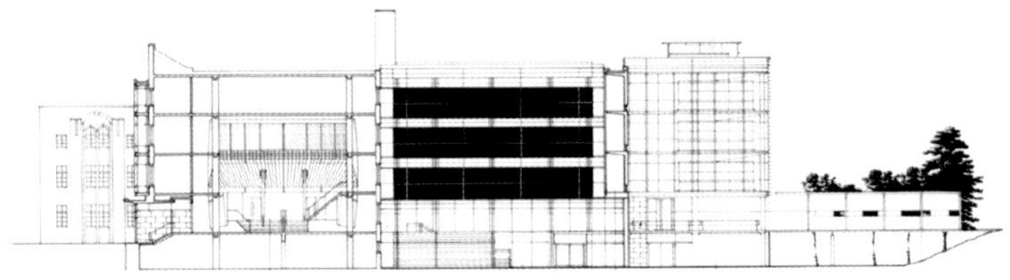

Architects	**Saucier + Perrotte / Menkès Shooner Dagenais**
Client	**Université de Montréal**
Completed	**1997**
Address	**2940 Chemin de la Côte-Sainte-Catherine**
Métro	**Université-de-Montréal**
Access	**university hours**

HEC MONTRÉAL

Affiliated with the Université de Montréal, the École des hautes études commerciales de Montréal underwent a massive growth spurt in the early 1990s with the surge of students wanting to become part of *Québec Inc.*, as the movement to Quebec-owned and -run businesses was described. The choice of site for the business school was controversial not only because it implied destruction of some untouched woodlands on the sloping south side of Cote Ste. Catherine but also because of the scale of the insertion into the neighbourhood. At 44,550 square metres, the building is often compared to an ocean liner berthed on the periphery of the campus.

The interior of HEC Montréal is large scale but coherent. The resolutely linear circulation draws the visitor to the centre of the building. Functions are stacked vertically: classrooms are on the first floor, the library on the second and offices on the floors above.

At the heart of the ground floor, a three-storey-high winter garden is the public space with cafeteria, gallery and meeting rooms. A surprising west wall, entirely glazed, curves into the plan as if to leave room for the trees beyond.

Natural light pours down cylindrical clerestories all the way from the seventh floor, infusing the core of the building with light.

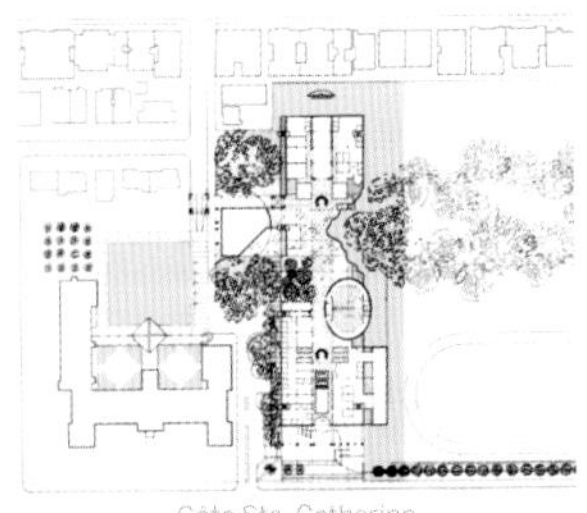

Architects	**Dan S. Hanganu / Jodoin Lamarre Pratte et Associés**
Client	**Université de Montréal**
Completed	**1996**
Address	**3000 Chemin de la Côte-Ste-Catherine**
Métro	**Université-de-Montréal**
Access	**university hours**

PAVILLON J.-ARMAND-BOMBARDIER DE L'ÉCOLE POLYTECHNIQUE

Buildings on the main campus of the Université de Montréal are required to be clad in the yellow brick used by Ernest Cormier for the iconic central pavilion in 1942. Here the north and west sides of the Bombardier pavilion face towards the central campus, their pale-yellow brick alternating with horizontal bands of glazing that allow natural light into offices. Charcoal-colour brick on the south and east indicates the core block of laboratories.

The building houses an interdisciplinary group of science and engineering researchers from the École Polytechnique and the Université de Montréal. Setting the offices at the perimeter and wrapping them around the laboratory block is a deceptively simple solution to a complex program that must meet the very diverse needs of seven hundred researchers.

The sobriety of the exterior belies the richness of the interior. Natural light pours through the oversized windows, and a series of small lounges, where people may gather to exchange ideas or eat and lunch, punctuates the perimeter. The orange-metal-clad atrium – five metres wide and five storeys high – is a connector and a brilliant unexpected slice of colour.

To the north and downhill from the Bombardier pavilion, the 2005 Pavillons Lassonde by Saia Barbarese Topouzanov / Desnoyers Mercure / MSDL architects are LEED gold-certified buildings in which departments of the École Polytechnique are located. They are noteworthy for their use of colour in the interior as a system of identification.

Architects	**Provencher Roy et Associés / Desnoyers Mercure et Associés / Menkès Shooner Dagenais**
Client	**École Polytechnique**
Completed	**2004**
Address	**Chemin de Polytechnique**
Métro	**Université-de-Montréal**
Access	**university hours**

LES PROJETS EUROPA, PHASE IV

In an industrial sector of Outremont adjoining the railway tracks, a series of intriguing housing projects was built by the same developer in five successive phases over five years. The project revitalized a part of the *quartier* in a language and scale consistent with the neighbourhood. Each phase is relatively modest in size and scope, and each is a variant on a different housing typology. Phase I on Querbes consists of eight townhouses, and Phase II on De l'Épée is a mix of three-storey and single-storey units. The two phases back onto the same laneway, accessible via a *porte-cochère* on De l'Épée, in traditional Montreal fashion.

The most overtly industrial project is Phase IV, which reuses the two steel structures of a former laundry at the southwest corner of De l'Épée and Ducharme. Each of the two volumes that comprise the project – thirty apartments in total – fronts onto the two streets. Units at ground level have their own entrances. A central courtyard uses the remnants of the steel structure as the base for a system of bridges and balconies for the exterior circulation system that is at once adventurous and appropriate.

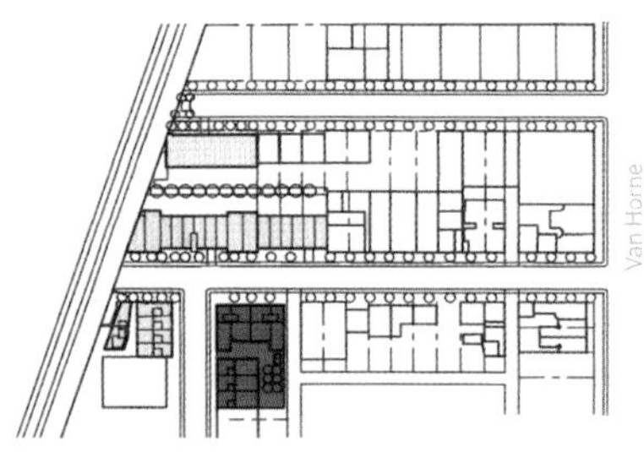

Architects	**Boutros + Pratte**
Client	**Jean-Pierre Houle**
Completed	**2001**
Address	**1100-1150 Av. Ducharme**
Métro	**Outremont**
Access	**exterior only**

Fielding
Parc de la Confédération
Parc Somerled
Somerled
Randall
Cumberland
Bessborough
Borden
Côte-Saint-Luc
Terrebonne
Parc Benny
Complexe sportif de Notre-Dame-de-Grâce
Grand
Royal
Harvard
Girouard
Monkland
Métro Villa-Maria
Centre culturel de Notre-Dame-de-Grâce
Benny Farm
Notre-Dame-de-Grâce
Cavendish
Benny
Sherbrooke
Côte-Saint-Antoine
Parc Notre-Dame-de-Grâce
De Maisonneuve
Décarie
Upper-Lachine
Métro Vendôme
Saint-Jacques
Autoroute Décarie
Pullman
Autoroute Ville-Marie
0
400 metres
4 minutes to walk

NOTRE DAME DE GRÂCE

NDG, as this borough of the City of Montreal is known, was melon farms and apple orchards until the latter part of the 19th century. A village located on Décarie between Côte St. Antoine and Notre Dame de Grâce, at the easternmost edge of present-day NDG, served the farms. Institutional presence around the original village is still very evident: many of the convents and monasteries owned by various religious orders were converted to other uses in the 1990s – principally condominiums – with very mixed results architecturally. The character of eastern NDG had, however, already been dramatically transformed by the 1967 construction of the depressed Décarie expressway.

At the turn of the 20th century, tramways provided access to and from a growing downtown. The new suburb was built almost entirely in the forty-year period prior to the Second World War – a mix of semi-detached single-family houses to the north, duplexes to the south and walk-up apartments along Sherbrooke, the principal commercial artery.

At the western border of NDG, Concordia University's Loyola College campus was built by the Jesuits to serve the English Catholic community in 1916. Contemporary additions to Concordia include the Richard J. Renaud Building (2003) by Marosi + Troy / Jodoin Lamarre Pratte et associés / Cardinal Hardy.

The MUHC (McGill University Health Centre), completed in 2015 on the former Glen railway yards at the southeastern corner of NDG, regroups five different institutions. This super-hospital is a major intervention in the *quartier*, as is its counterpart, the CHUM (Centre hospitalier de l'université de Montréal) in the Quartier Latin; their impact will have to be evaluated.

BENNY FARM

Built in 1947 to house Second World War veterans and their families, a series of brick three-storey walk-ups was spread over two super-blocks on a 7.3-hectare site. By the early 1990s, the buildings were aging and no longer meeting the residents' needs. However, discussion about how to redevelop the site as a whole, to be appropriate in form and in use to the community – including how to reuse some of the existing buildings – lasted more than twelve years. Community involvement in the project remained remarkably strong throughout the process, which culminated in a task force in 2002.

Four architectural firms participated in the Task Force. Saia Barbarese Topouzanov was given the mandate in 2003 to develop the site plan. Their solution provided the oversized blocks with private and semi-public spaces neatly defined by pedestrian streets; Claude Cormier's landscape plan retained the community garden at the heart of the block.

Architects	**Saia Barbarese Topouzanov (master plan)**
Landscape architect	**Claude Cormier (master plan)**
Client	**Canada Lands Company, CMHC and others**
Completed	**1996 – 2007**
Address	**Rues Monkland and Sherbrooke between Walkley and Benny**
Métro	**Vendôme (+ bus 105 ouest) or Villa-Maria (+ bus 162 ouest)**
Access	**exterior only**

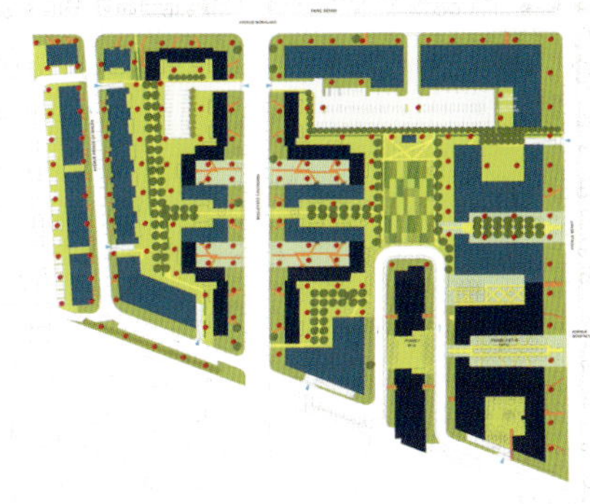

BENNY FARM

Les Habitations Benny Farm

Saia Barabarese designed Les Habitations Benny Farm, an elegant apartment block for veterans, which is orange-brick clad with pixelated green glass-wrapped balconies. Anthracite-coloured stucco on the interior face of the two buildings defines the more private courtyard side.

Claude Cormier's landscape design for Les Habitations Benny Farm includes visually rich interior courtyards that layer hard surface and vegetation, private and public spaces.

Architects	**Saia Barbarese / Laverdière + Giguêre**
Landscape architect	**Claude Cormier**
Client	**Canada Lands Company**
Completed	**2000**
Address	**Rue Benny and 3700 and 3800 Veterans Lane**
Métro	**Vendôme (+ bus 105 ouest) or Villa-Maria (+ bus 162 ouest)**
Access	**exterior only**

Chez Soi

L'OEUF, an architectural firm that had participated in the Benny Farm process from the beginning, designed Chez Soi, affordable housing for seniors on Cavendish. The six-storey brick building's glazed ground floor space is like a front porch on the neighbourhood. Built according to sustainable principles, the building is heated by a combination of heat sources including solar and geothermal.

L'OEUF has been responsible for the recycling and rebuilding of three other existing buildings on Benny Farm: two housing cooperatives and housing for young mothers.

Architects	**L'OEUF**
Owners	**Chez Soi**
Completed	**2006**
Address	**3825 Cavendish**
Métro	**Vendôme (+ bus 105 ouest) or Villa Maria (+ bus 162 ouest)**
Access	**exterior only**

BENNY PARK

Complexe sportif de Notre-Dame-de-Grâce

The desire to reduce the impact of the structure on the environment in every way is evident in the green-roofed Complexe sportif NDG, partly submerged into Benny Park. Designed to be sustainable in both its construction and its operation, it maintained the greatest amount of the park's green space possible – in direct response to the concerns of the people who live in the neighbourhood – and that is its strength.

Architects **Consortium Thibodeau Poirier Fontaine**
Client **Arrondissement Côte-des-Neiges / Notre-Dame-de-Grâce**
Completed **2011**
Address **6445 Av. Monkland**
Métro **Vendôme (+ bus 105 ouest)**
Access **see website**

Centre culturel Notre-Dame-de-Grâce

The significance of this library, cultural centre and community space lies not only in its use but in the deliberate gesture of its location. As in many other *quartiers* in Montreal, a new node has been created that pivots around culture and/or sports – here the components are the Centre culturel, the Complexe sportif opposite and the CLSC, a local community services health centre immediately to the west. There is a deeper connection still to Benny Farm, as the cultural centre sits firmly on the northeast corner of the block.

The result of a 2010 architectural competition, the building is all colour and openness, about movement from one level of the building to another, from inside to outside. There's nothing shy or retiring about the centre; it makes it clear that it has arrived in the neighbourhood.

Architects	**Atelier Big City / Fichten Soiferman / L'OEUF**
Landscape architects	**NIPpaysage**
Client	**Arrondissement Côte-des-Neiges / Notre-Dame-de-Grâce**
Completed	**2016**
Address	**6400 Av. Monkland**
Métro	**Vendôme (+ bus 105 ouest)**
Access	**see website**

Autoroute Ville-Marie
Saint-Antoine
Métro Georges-Vanier
Coursol
Place Saint-Henri
Couvent
Dominion
Georges-Vanier
Saint-Martin
Richmond
Guy
Métro Lionel-Groulx
Saint-Jacques
Vinet
Métro Place-Saint-Henri
Lionel-Groulx
Delisle
Les Habitations Georges-Vanier
des Seigneurs
Greene
Atwater
Workman
Saint-Augustin
Turgeon
Bourget
Rose-de-Lima
Irène
Notre-Dame
Canning
Centre sportif de la Petite-Bourgogne
1700 La Poste
Saint-Ferdinand
Marché Atwater
Duvernay
Sainte-Émilie
Habitations Turgeon
Habitations St-Ambroise
Résidence St-Ambroise
Habitations St-Ambroise
Rufus-Rockhead
Sainte-Cunégonde
Canal de Lachine
DentsuBos
Saint-Ambroise
des Éclusiers
Canal de Lachine
Saint-Patrick
Augustin-Cantin
Lofts Redpath
Allez-up
Métro Charlevoix
Centre
Charlevoix
Grand Trunk
0
200 metres

ST. HENRI / LACHINE CANAL / LITTLE BURGUNDY

Canada's premier industrial heritage site, the Lachine Canal, was built in 1825 to link the Montreal harbour to Lac St. Louis, bypassing the Lachine Rapids and allowing navigation to penetrate the North American continent. The canal was used continuously until 1970, when the 1959 St. Lawrence Seaway became the sole route for ships.

The canal was the cradle of industry in Canada; refineries, mills and factories lined its banks in the mid-19th century, as they used the canal not only to ship their goods but as a source of hydraulic power. The neighbourhoods on both sides of the canal were built up in the latter part of the 19th century as housing for those who worked in the factories. To the south of the canal, Point St. Charles was dominated by railway yards; to the north, St. Henri and Little Burgundy were a mix of residential and industrial.

The fourteen-kilometre-long canal and its banks are now a linear park, owned and maintained as a historic site by Parks Canada, and restored as a navigable waterway in 2002.

Recycling of industrial structures along the canal started in the mid-1980s with the conversion of the former Stelco steel plant and the Belding-Corticelli silk mill into condominiums. Recession in the 1990s slowed conversion and new construction was almost non-existent, but from 2000 onwards, condominiums sprouted like mushrooms, concentrating first around the Atwater Market.

Revitalization is not without cost, however; planning the mix of condos and affordable housing necessary to maintain the essence of these *quartiers* has not always been successful.

RUE SAINT-AMBROISE

Rue St. Ambroise is at the southern limit of St. Henri bordering the Lachine Canal, the site of 19th-century factories and mills. Revitalization started slowly in the early 1990s, with conversion of industrial buildings for artists' studios and lofts – new construction was limited to houses built by architects for themselves.

Neatly occupying the corner, the four-level single-family house at 70 Rose-de-Lima is inserted into a tightly constrained lot at the intersection with St. Ambroise. Its subdued, simple language and stucco cladding set it apart from the vernacular of the neighbourhood. Interiors are open plan, organized around a central staircase.

On the east side of Rose-de-Lima, on a triangular site bought from the City of Montreal, immediately opposite the Atwater Market, Les habitations Saint-Ambroise attracted attention from the start. Its site, its construction in the mid-1990s, when little or no construction was going on in Montreal, and its adherence to sustainable principles set it apart. Definitely not the typical linear Montreal housing type, its four units are stacked and sorted vertically. All living and sleeping spaces are housed on the first and second floors. The ground floor is reserved for studios, garages and offices.

Résidence Saint-Ambroise

70 Rue Rose-de-Lima

Architects **Fortin / Shoiry**
Completed **1992**
Métro **Lionel-Groulx**

Les habitations Saint-Ambroise

81 Rue Rose-de-Lima

Architects **L'OEUF**
Completed **1996**
Métro **Lionel-Groulx**

As living on the banks of the Lachine Canal became fashionable in the late 1990s, a series of condominiums was built in rapid succession, particularly in the stretch near the Atwater Market. The seven-unit construction at 3701 to 3711 St. Ambroise set itself apart by carrying on the adventurous spirit of the earlier houses on Rose-de-Lima. Each unit reads like an individual address. Materials vary from red brick to shiplapped zinc shingles, and glazing is generous. A second project by Affleck + de la Riva in the next block west uses colour and distinctly contemporary fenestration that leaves one guessing as to the layout of the seven units inside. It takes the best possible advantage of the park across the street, which allows unobstructed views of the canal.

Farther west on St. Ambroise, the principal structure in the Merchants' Manufacturing complex was built in 1880 for textile production and was one of the first conversions to offices and studios in the early 1990s. A wing and a subsequent annex were transformed for use as offices for the advertising firm DentsuBos by architect Luc Laporte. The box-like annex was entirely clad in copper shingles, giving it a presence both on the canal side and from the street.

Les Habitations Saint-Ambroise

3701–3711 Rue Saint-Ambroise

Architects **Affleck + de la Riva**
Completed **2003**
Métro **Lionel-Groulx**

Les Habitations Turgeon

3741 Rue Saint-Ambroise

Architects **Affleck + de la Riva**
Completed **2013**
Métro **Lionel-Groulx**

DentsuBos

3970 Rue Saint-Ambroise

Architects **Luc Laporte**
Completed **2007**
Métro **Place-Saint-Henri**

LES CONDOS IRÈNE

Converting industrial buildings to residential is an ongoing process in St. Henri, and the design decision in every case is how the contemporary manifests itself. In Irène, it is very clear – three new storeys have been added on top of the original two-storey 1938 building, wrapped in a perforated aluminum cladding. The intent, according to the architects, was to create a lighter volume that floated above the existing building. The modular panels create a curtain that changes constantly as residents open and close the shutters.

The risk in a gesture like this is that the building overwhelms its surroundings. To its credit, Irène sits very neatly at its street corner with commercial spaces on St. Jacques.

On the western side of Irène, architects Vladimir and Nadejda Topouzanov reclad an early-20th-century triplex in 2007 in a bouquet of coloured brick that is a visual treat.

Architects	**KANVA**
Client	**3745 Saint-Jacques Inc.**
Completed	**2012**
Address	**701 Rue Sainte-Irène**
Métro	**Lionel-Groulx**
Access	**exterior only**

LACHINE CANAL

The massive project to revitalize the canal was realized over the seven-year period from 1997 to 2004. The principal players were Parks Canada (a federal agency), the City of Montreal and other municipalities that border the canal's length – working in concert with community and heritage groups.

The primary focus has been on encouraging recreational use in the linear park, using the traces of the industrial history as a narrative. Restoration work was extensive and included rebuilding the masonry walls and restoring the locks, which permitted the reopening of the canal as a navigable waterway in 2002.

The St. Gabriel locks at Charlevoix are the strongest vestiges of the working canal and also a node for conversion of industrial buildings. Contemporary intervention in this project is most evident in the area around Atwater Market. A pedestrian bridge connects the bike path on the south side of the canal to a small public square (Schème) and service pavilion by Lapointe Magne, completed in 2002.

Architects/Client	**Parks Canada / Ville de Montréal / Société du Vieux-Port de Montréal**
Completed	**2004**
Address	**14.5 km between the Old Port and Lac Saint-Louis**
Métro	**Lionel-Groulx or Charlevoix**
Access	**public**

Lofts Redpath

The most significant industrial complex on the Lachine Canal, the Redpath Sugar Refinery, closed in 1979 and stood derelict for twenty years. Its conversion to condominiums in three phases from 2000 to 2007 was controversial, as some Montrealers would have preferred a cultural use and the intervention was subject to much scrutiny. The exoskeleton of stairways on the courtyard side is the most compelling part of the new construction. The courtyard allows access to commercial spaces at grade, including a two-storey wing fronting onto a dock.

Architects	**Cardinal Hardy**
Owner	**Société immobilière Gueymard**
Completed	**2007**
Address	**1721 Rue Saint-Patrick**
Métro	**Charlevoix (+ bus 107)**
Access	**exterior only**

Allez-up

Two of four silos that were once part of the Redpath Sugar Refinery form the backdrop of a rock climbing centre. The entry to the centre uses the base of one of the silos, but the interior full height of the silo is not visible; the climbing wall determined the shape and volume of the contemporary metal-clad structure, gashed by irregular windows. Reuse of the silos is not a small task – the centre's incremental approach is at once playful and appropriate.

Architects **Smith Vigeant**
Owner **Jean-Marc de la Plante**
Completed **2012**
Address **1555 Rue Saint-Patrick**
Métro **Charlevoix (+ bus 107)**
Access **see website**

LES HABITATIONS GEORGES-VANIER

Winner of a 1991 pan-Canadian competition, *L'art de vivre en ville*, organized to seek out "original, functional and flexible designs" for families buying a first home in the downtown area, this project takes the traditional Montreal duplex and gives it a deliberate twist. Ten units form what is called a *tête d'ilôt*, an ensemble that terminates a block. The outside stairways are a recognizable feature of Montreal housing, but the form and materials set this row resolutely apart. (The grey concrete block was originally conceived by de la Riva to be clad in stucco, evoking the 1930s, but this was overruled by the City.) Each unit consists of a two-bedroom apartment on the ground floor and a larger two-storey maisonette above it. Patios at grade and roof terraces provide private outdoor space for both residences. The path and courtyard behind are communal space.

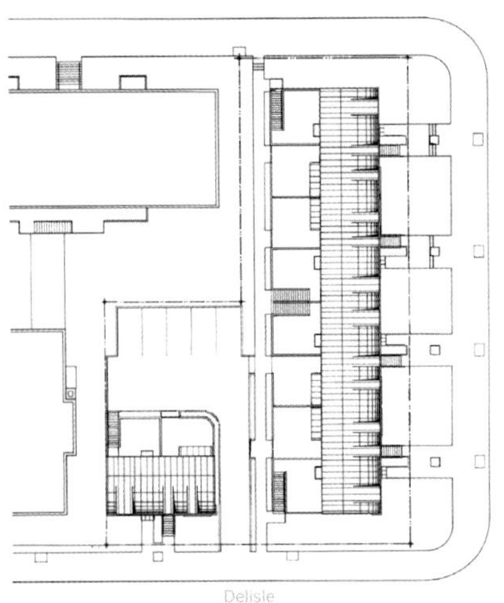

Architects	**Richard de la Riva**
Client	**Ville de Montréal**
Completed	**1993**
Address	**corner Boul. Georges-Vanier and Av. Delisle**
Métro	**Georges-Vanier**
Access	**exterior only**

CENTRE SPORTIF DE LA PETITE-BOURGOGNE

The Centre sportif de la Petite-Bourgogne is a community sports facility on an old street in a working-class neighbourhood. The building is simple, understandable, robust and at a scale that is completely appropriate to its street-corner site. Two brick volumes – red for the gymnasium and anthracite for the swimming pool – sit on either side of an interior street. The stone-paved street follows the course of an old laneway and runs from Notre-Dame to a pedestrian path and schoolyard.

Colour and light are everywhere, and the relationship of inside to outside, particularly the pool to the park, is a delight. The simplicity of the materials is deceptive. Closer inspection reveals an attention to detail that is rare in a building constructed on a relatively modest budget.

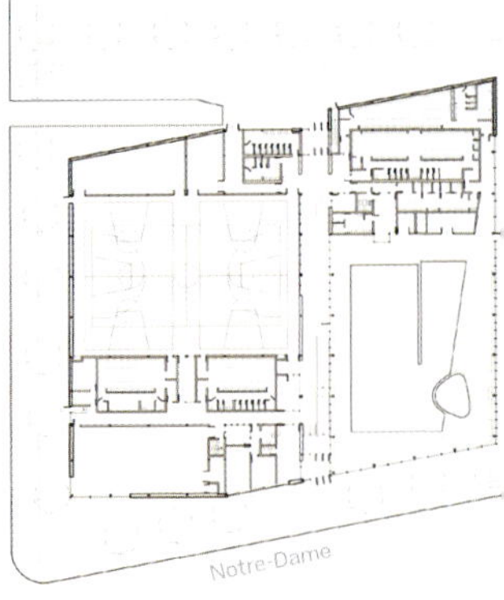

Architects **Saia Barbarese**
Client **Ville de Montréal**
Completed **1997**
Address **1825 Rue Notre-Dame Ouest (corner of Rue des Seigneurs)**
Métro **Georges-Vanier**
Access **public**

1700 LA POSTE

Reuse of existing buildings is a major part of most Montreal architects' practices – every intervention possible, from meticulous restoration to swallowing buildings whole. The transformation of David Jerome Spence's 1913 Postal Station F into art space is not evident from the exterior, though it has clearly been cleaned and polished. The interior is the contemporary gesture, one that reflects the original public character of the post office and its Beaux arts language. The exhibition space is white but not anonymous – it's assured and solidly detailed.

The element that really sets the project apart, however, is the ensemble that sits under the mezzanine. Ticket counter, cloakroom and bar are all built into a wood assembly that is conceived and built like a beautifully executed piece of furniture.

Architects	**Luc Laporte**
Client	**Isabelle de Mévius**
Completed	**2014**
Address	**1700 Rue Notre-Dame Ouest**
Métro	**Georges-Vanier**
Access	**see website**

EXIT

Abélard
Parc
Elgar
La Station
Berlioz
Boulevard de l'Île-des-Sœurs
Corot
Wilson
Elgar
Darwin
Parc de
West Vancouver
Fleuve Saint-Laurent
0
100 metres
1 minute to walk

VERDUN / ÎLE DES SOEURS

222 LA STATION – MAISON INTERGÉNÉRATIONNELLE

Agricultural until the middle of the 19th century, Verdun is defined by the aqueduct to the north and the St. Lawrence River to the south. Flooding delayed residential development until a dyke was built; in the early 20th century, small builders built out the neighbourhood rapidly and densely. Always known as a workers' neighbourhood, it was and remains primarily residential, with the exception of the Douglas Hospital and its extensive grounds that also provide public green space.

Île des Soeurs (Nuns' Island) was annexed to Verdun in 1956, having been owned and farmed by the religious community of the Soeurs de la Congregation de Notre-Dame until that time. With the 1962 construction of the Champlain Bridge linking the new expressways on the island of Montreal to the south shore of the St. Lawrence, there was finally a connection between Île des Soeurs and Verdun.

Metropolitan Structures from Chicago leased and developed the island according to a master plan by Johnson, Johnson & Roy of Ann Arbour, Michigan, a firm responsible for planning many American university campuses. Planned as a model community, it very skillfully mixed heights and volumes in a "cluster" layout that provided a series of small-scale green spaces and pedestrian-only access. Of their original fifteen-year, eight-phase plan, four phases were built, including a shopping centre, community centre, school and golf course in an extraordinary natural environment. Metropolitan stopped development in 1978, and other developers built out the rest of the island.

Mies van der Rohe had worked with Metropolitan Structures in Baltimore and Detroit. On Île des Soeurs, he was responsible for the concept of three residential towers on the river's edge (the first with architect Philip Bobrow of Montreal and the second and third with architect Edgar Tornay) and the unique Esso service station.

LA STATION – MAISON INTERGÉNÉRATIONNELLE

A component of the original Île des Sœurs community, the service station was designed for Esso by Mies van der Rohe in 1967–68, in association with Montreal architect Paul Lapointe. The plan was simplicity itself, in the language of the pavilion that marks so much of Mies's work: two glass boxes – one a service bay for mechanics and one a customer service space – linked by a flat roof built on black I-beams. The gas pumps were located on an island between the two volumes.

Closed in 2008, the station was cited as a building of heritage value by the City of Montreal a year later. While reusing the station as an intergenerational community centre was seen as a good choice, it was clear that the transformation would not be easy. Éric Gauthier of FABG edited the Mies station, paring it down to its essence and giving each of the two volumes a slightly different character. The seniors' space has a white floor, the youth space a black floor; both have tightly contained storage units that house equipment. Where the gas pumps once stood, cleverly designed air intakes serve the geothermal heating system.

Architects **FABG**
Client **Arrondissement de Verdun**
Completed **2011**
Address **201 Rue Berlioz**
Métro **Square-Victoria–OACI (+ bus 168 sud)**
Access **exterior only**

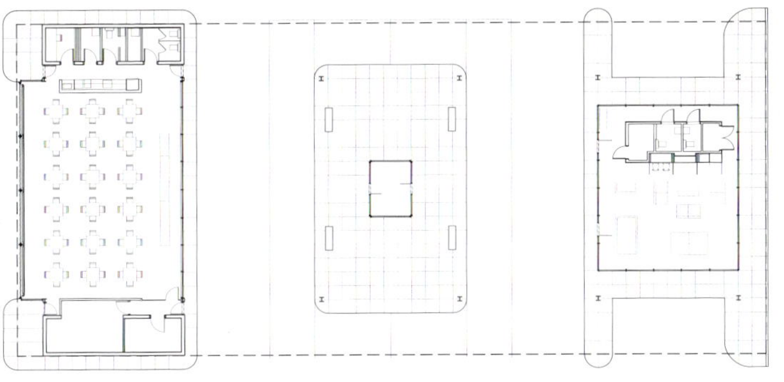

ONE SUNDAY OVER LUNCH

Ricardo L. Castro and Martin Houle in Conversation

Ricardo L. Castro, associate professor at the School of Architecture at McGill University, and Martin Houle, architect and founder of Kollectif, a Quebec web-based organization that promotes communication within all the design communities, sat down one sunny Sunday over lunch to talk about architecture in Montreal. Here are some of their thoughts in answer to our questions:

What is the new generation of architects up to?

Martin: The new generation of architects is doing the kind of quick-win projects like Bellastock. Bellastock was an international movement that started in France, and now they have some in Turkey and some in China and everywhere in the world. And a lot of French students came to Montreal and they brought that notion of Bellastock and said, "Well, there's no Bellastock section here, so why don't we start one?"

And through social media, they got people around and they were saying, "Okay, well, we'll use these construction materials that are left over, and we'll do something." And so sometimes it's these sub-organizations that initiate something, like Pecha Kucha. It was an international kind of infrastructure and it was adapted to Montreal, and it worked very well for a while.

Well, the subculture became culture. It may not be in New York. It may not be in Paris or whatever, but maybe Montreal was a boiling pot of things about to be, and just all of a sudden it's popping up.

How are citizens getting involved in the city?

Martin: They should have the last word on what's going on, but there's that whole other issue of while having involved citizens is good – getting the feedback – as professionals, what do we do? What's our place in that? So it's getting very, very interesting.

Ricardo: I've seen people, ordinary citizens – not architects – being in a building or being in a place. They are looking at something or experiencing it, and feeling, "Oh, wow, this is amazing." Already, that is an engagement that is very important, the wow. When you go by the Saucier + Perrotte stadium, right, and it's a wow.

What's the role of social media in architecture these days?

Martin: It's like any new tool. I mean, it's like when concrete came, it was a new tool and it goes to one extreme, and after, it comes back. Social media's really the same thing; it's going to one extreme and now people are having an overdose.

And when you look, for example, at the Kollectif newsletter, before the importance of it was because there was a lack of information gathering. Now, it's actually a "best of" because there's so much information. But one of the things that social media is doing is putting people together.

You know, we were talking about schools as infrastructure community centres. In the past, the will was there, but there was no infrastructure for communication. Now, with social media, the infrastructure is there, so therefore things flow and things get made

Is the current generation of architects more mobile?

Martin: I think what marks the next generation of architects and designers is mobility in every sense of the word. Mobility in terms of being able to work on a common project – going elsewhere in the world or whatever.

Ricardo: Physical mobility, I think, is playing a very important role. I see it in some of my students. I just talked to one yesterday – he just went to London and he decided to stay there. He was in Berlin – there he found this exposure also to all these incredible things that are happening in some other places. I feel that, in a way, the exposure will be reflected in what these people are going to be doing. I hope so.

Do young architects feel a connection to the city?

Ricardo: I cannot speak for everybody, but I think there is a certain concern, and one of the ways I see it happening, more and more, is like the projects that are proposed at the level of the master's or even the projects in the undergraduate studios. And I see that there is more concern now for having a direct involvement with the city.

What do you think being a UNESCO City of Design has done for Montreal?

Martin: There was the whole issue at one point about the designation of Montreal as a UNESCO City of Design and people were misinterpreting the message behind it – it's not a recognition.

It's saying that Montreal has that subculture. Montreal has that talent, and I think that right now it's a great time to be a designer in Montreal, because things are happening. Very interesting things are happening, and I'm very positive for the next five, ten, fifteen years.

Is there a particular scale that Montreal architects have mastered?

Ricardo: The question is quite interesting. Why is it that these things happen here? Why is it that Montreal, unlike many other places, is not characterized by this desire to build big grand scales of things? And, you know, we see the towers but those are in no way symbolic . . .

I'm going to come back to the idea of the landscape. But I come more to the idea of "place," and I think that the idea of creating places, humanized places, in the city, within the city and connected to it has become a preoccupation that architects have nowadays.

The more I see things, the more I realize that we find in the city the idea of shakkei, or Japanese borrowed view. It is a communion that is wonderful, no?

Martin: Well, one of the interesting discussions that I've had many times is what's Montreal's trademark in architecture? And nobody really can define something. A lot of architects are looking to the Scandinavians, for example, and saying, "Maybe it'll be the wood buildings. Maybe it'll be something like that." But what marks Montreal from a tectonic or from a design or formal point of view as signature?

What I think does characterize Montreal is that there's a whole level of multidisciplinary openness to one another that you might not find in a lot of cities. It's a community-based thing: small-scale projects where you've got graphic designers, interior designers, architects working together in a way that maybe you won't see in another city.

What do you think of the new libraries being designed and built in Montreal?

Ricardo: You know, this reminds me of Colombia. It reminds me of Bogota. It reminds me of the mayor, Peñalosa, who came up with the idea twenty years ago, "Let's make libraries," and he made, all over Bogota, a series of satellite libraries. Some of them were renovations, so for instance an old place that used to be a trash processing plant became a library.

Then someone was commissioned to make one, so they started appearing, but it was a concerted effort and of course there are political reasons for that. But here with the competitions, there's a similar thing happening . . . which gathers very good projects, and unfortunately sometimes some are not so great, but . . .

Martin: So with all the competitions that the City of Montreal has been doing for libraries, there's the whole question of why libraries, now that we have the internet? And there's that whole discussion of saying, "Well, maybe now libraries are not those places where you don't talk anymore. They're places for people to connect. Instead of always just being in your apartment and working, you say, "Let's meet at the library and talk and have a coffee."

How optimistic are you?

Ricardo: It's interesting that you have mentioned this notion of optimism, which I must say, fifteen years ago I didn't have it, and twenty years ago I did not have it at all. I even remember writing something saying there was no future. Now, I think the city's offering that opportunity. A lot of things that are happening, you know, sporadically here and there, I see that crossing through the city. I feel it when I walk through a *quartier*. It's a sense that, "Oh, my gosh. It is really getting better and better."

Do you feel that Montreal has been in a good place over the past eight years in terms of architecture and design and urban design?

Ricardo: I feel that it has. I want more.

A 2008 agreement between Quebec and the City of Montreal included a program intended to renovate, enlarge and construct libraries in Montreal's boroughs. Architectural competitions were organized by the Bureau du Design de Montréal; five projects have been completed or are in construction, including a new library in Pierrefonds to be built by 2017.

Bibliothèque du Boisé

An almost flamboyant use of space makes the exterior a little overblown and the transparency towards the woods to the north that the library is named for could be stronger. The strength of the project lies in the node it is creating in the community and in its details.

Architects	**Cardinal Hardy / Labonté Mercier / Éric Pelletier**
Client	**Arrondissement de Saint-Laurent**
Completed	**2013**
Address	**2727 Boul. Thimens**
Métro	**Côte Vertu (+ bus 171 ouest)**
Access	**see website**

Bibliothèque Saul-Bellow

Clean, white, crisp and easy to read, the new library has subsumed the original 1975 building in the best possible way. Providing the whole range of services the contemporary library now must offer, it does so on a relatively constrained site.

Architects	**Chevalier Morales**
Client	**Arrondissement de Lachine**
Completed	**2015**
Address	**3100 Rue St. Antoine ouest**
Métro	**Lionel-Groulx (+ bus 496 ouest)**
Access	**see website**

INDEX BY BUILDING / PUBLIC SPACE

INDEX BY ARCHITECT

INDEX BY BUILDING TYPE

CREDITS

All architectural drawings are reproduced courtesy of the architects with the exception of:

Maison Coloniale which is included with the kind permission of the Fonds Jacques Rousseau, Canadian Centre for Architecture, Montreal.

Canadian Centre for Architecture which is included courtesy of the Peter Rose fonds, Canadian Centre for Architecture, Montreal, Gift of Peter Rose.

Unless otherwise indicated, the photographs were created by the architects themselves or commissioned by each firm. We have made every effort to locate and list the copyright for all illustrations. Where the credit is not listed, it is either held by the architect or we have been unable to determine the copyright holder, in which case we would ask that person to contact the publisher.

Photographers' credits:

Marie-Christine Abel. 85
Tom Arban. 33 bottom, 38, 39 top, 48, 49, 51
© BAnQ, Bernard Fougères. 149 bottom left
Louis Bellefleur. 46, 55 top
Olivier Blouin. 185 bottom
James Brittain. 108, 109, 203 right
Stéphane Brügger. 67, 114, 133, 202
Michel Brunelle. 53, 55 bottom, 86, 141, 145, 151, 168, 169, 177, 180, 181, 191 bottom
Canadian Centre for Architecture, Montreal. 35, 37 top and bottom right
Marc Cramer. 33 top, 39 bottom right, 57 bottom right, 61 top, 63, 77, 87, 92, 95, 134, 135, 192, 193, 207 middle, 209
Roderick Chen. 105
Pierre Desjardins. 125, 164, 165
doublespace. 230
James Dow. 149 top and bottom right
Robert Etcheverry. 96, 106, 159 right, 195, 207 left
Denis Farley. 113, 115, 117, 200
Fonds Jacques Rousseau, Canadian Centre for Architecture, Montreal. 157
Wayne Fujii. 41
Stéphane Groleau. 68, 69, 107
Alain Laforest. 39 bottom left, 40, 57 top and bottom left, 64, 65 top, 72, 73, 75, 76, 79, 80, 81, 89, 91, 93, 97, 116, 121, 138, 139, 147 top, 153 top and bottom left, 158, 172, 183, 185 top, 203 left, 206, 207 right, 211, 216, 217, 218
Alain Lefort. 219
Jean-François Lenoir. 215
Matt Makauskas. 198, 199
Jean Mercier. 47
Brian Merrett, MMFA. 30, 31
Steve Montpetit. 126, 127, 130, 131, 163, 178, 179, 223
Benoit Muyldemans. 171 top
Éric Piché. 147 bottom left and right, 189
Richard Poissant. 191 top
Nikkol Rot. 171 bottom
Fiona Spalding-Smith. 29
Michel Tremblay. 161
Jean-François Vézina. 103
Vittorio Vieira. 212

Quartiers in the guidebook